THE Unexplained

Strange Talents

People who can see the future, heal the sick and communicate with the dead

Editor: Peter Brookesmith

CHARTWELL
BOOKS, INC.

Acknowledgements
Photographs were supplied by Aberdeen Journals, AGIP, Aldus Book, Aldus/Field Museum of Natural History, Aldus/Warburg Institute, K.M. Andrews, Ashmoleum, Audio Ltd., Channel 9-Australian TV, Bettman Archive, Paul Brierley, BBC (Hulton) Picture Library, Dept. of Engineering Cambridge University, G. Chapman, Jean-Loup Charmet, Bruce Coleman, Colorific, Cliché Combier, John Cutten, René Dazy, Robert Estall, Mary Evans Picture Library, Joel Finler, Focus, Werner Forman Archive, FOT Library, Tom Smith/Fortrose Town Council, Frater Albertus/Paracelsus College/Salt Lake City, French Govt. Tourist Office, John Frost, Leif Geiges, Rose Gladden, John Glanville, Joan Grant, Hebridean Press Agency, Hertfordshire Echo & Post, Toby Hogarth, Michael Holford, Robert Hunt Picture Library, John Hughes, Inter-Photo, Alix Jeffrey, Kadima Productions Inc., Laphina, Beverley Lebarrow, MacMillan Publishers, Dr. J.A. Macrae, William MacQuitty, Mansell Collection, Roger Mayne, Guy Lyon Playfair, Photri, Coral Polge, Popperfoto, Press Association, Psychic News Psycho Physical Research Foundation, Henry Puharich, Rex Features, Roger-Viollet, Routledge & Kegan Paul, Royal Collection, Royal Commission on Ancient & Historical Monuments of Scotland, Scala, Ronald Sheridan Photo Library, Paul Snelgrove, Spectrum Colour Library, Sphere Books, Sri Sathya Sai Baba Trust, Roy Stemman, Syndication International, John Topham Picture Library, Tyne Tees TV, UPI, ZEFA.

Consultants:
Professor A J Ellinson
Dr J Allen Hynek
Brian Inglis
Colin Wilson

Contents

Introduction

ONE OF THE REASONS why almost everyone is intrigued by the paranormal is that almost everyone has had some experience of it, no matter how slight. How many times have you had a relative – or a friend, or even a neighbour whom you may know only slightly – pop into your mind for no apparent reason, then had them telephone just a little while later – or write a letter which arrives in the next mail? This kind of thing happens often enough for most of us to suspect, at least, that something unusual is going on – that more than coincidence is at work. Yet, at the same time, most events like this are so trivial they don't stop us in our tracks either.

Some people however simply *can't* ignore their encounters with the paranormal. The things they experience are so remarkable – sometimes so disturbing – that they are forced to acknowledge that there are forces at work around them that they – along with everyone else – do not understand and often cannot control. Most people who discover that they can bend metal by means of psychokinesis, or hear the voices of the dead, or have premonitions of the future, find positive uses for their strange talents. But the way in which they first discover that talent can be something of a shock – indeed paranormality can manifest itself in its early stages quite differently from the way its energies may ultimately be used. The English psychic Matthew Manning, for instance, was first made aware of his strange talents by way of a massive outbreak of poltergeist activity that wrought havoc in his parents' house. As you can read in another volume in this series, he first channelled his psychic energy into an apparent ability to communicate with dead artists, producing some remarkable pictures as a result. Later he became adept at metal-bending, but by the early 1980s he had found his true vocation as a healer.

Others are introduced to their talents in less troubling ways, though often through a crisis or shock that triggers off an ability which may have been lying dormant until then. Psychic detective Gerard Croiset and clairaudient medium Doris Fisher Stokes discovered their abilities in this way. Tom Lethbridge, on the other hand, probably always had his remarkable capacity for dowsing, but had never had either the inclination or the opportunity to develop it until his retirement from academic life. The Scottish seer Kenneth Odhar would appear to have had his ability to see into the future all his life – though without his gift of prophecy the chances are his life would have been rather longer, and certainly not drastically curtailed in the way it was.

This inconsistency makes it all the more difficult to develop a theory as to the origins of such abilities. No less mysterious is the way in which some people's powers increase, are refined, or even change with time – or in some cases simply fade away. To some extent it is possible to suggest what kind of power is at work, in that a metal-bender like Uri Geller and a healer like Jose Arigo are both apparently using some form of psychokinesis (PK) – the ability to affect material things by mental effort alone – but to say that is really little more than saying we can put labels on *some* of the phenomena that occur. And even the labels we do have are precious little help when confronted by a medium like Doris Fisher Stokes or a – what? a magician? – such as Sai Baba.

In the case of Doris Stokes, opinion is divided between those who believe that she does exactly what she claims to do – hear the voices of the dead speaking from 'over there' – and those who believe that she is picking up, by telepathic means, information already in the mind of the person who wants to contact someone who has 'passed over'. To suggest that Doris Stokes is using telepathy does not, of course, mean that we should reject the idea that we survive bodily death: it is simply a question of what is really happening when Doris Stokes goes to work. When asked by the editorial team of this series whether she had considered the possibility that she *was*, in fact, reading the (unconscious) minds of her sitters, Doris Stokes replied that she would refuse to carry on her work if she felt she had been doing any such thing. 'That would be an invasion of privacy,' she said. 'I don't think God would allow that.' Nonetheless, the possibility remains that Doris Stokes is indeed highly telepathic, picking up memories from the mind of someone who knew the dead person. These memories are then dramatised by Mrs Stokes' own subconscious, and come to her in the form of voices. If her descriptions are anything to go by, they usually resemble the voice of the one who has passed on.

Presumably the reasons for this are two-fold. In the first place, Doris Stokes has that very strong resistance to the notion that she is invading other people's most private space – the mind. And, as you can read here, she has been utterly convinced that we *do* survive death. She cannot prevent her talent manifesting itself, and so has rationalised it in a way that has brought her, and thousands of people who have sat with her, great comfort. Even so, as we will see, such an explanation doesn't account for the remarkable way in which she first was made aware of her paranormal ability! On top of that, those of us who have seen Doris Stokes at work have no doubt that her abilities are indeed absolutely genuine – and very impressive.

There seems no reason to question the genuineness of guru Sai Baba, either. He has been investigated closely by representatives of the Society for Psychical Research, who could find no evidence of chicanery or sleight of hand – and no explanation of any other kind for Baba's production of apports. These range from holy ash, which he materialises by scooping it from the air or taking it from an empty urn, to fully formed medallions and even crucifixes (Baba reveres Christ as a prophet and redeemer). If that kind of activity can be labelled PK, it is PK of a very special kind. Mental control of physical reality is one thing: the capacity actually to *create* material objects seems to be of another order entirely. (If both phenomena seem too unlikely for comfort, it's worth remembering that every time you move a limb – walking to the kitchen because you've decided to make coffee for instance – you are proving that thought can affect the physical world. But there seems to be no simple equivalent like this to creating an apport.) It's scarcely surprising, then, that Sai Baba is regarded as a saint by many people – and not only in his own country; his following is world-wide. But while he may be a miracle man and a wise one at that, his particular kind of wisdom is little help in explaining his extraordinary feats – which set everything we thought we knew about the world on its ear. Sai Baba defeats the laws of space and time – *and* by all the evidence appears to be a reincarnation of another holy man.

This perplexing quality is common to many of the people described in these pages. To have abilities that fly in the face of common sense in just one respect would be unusual enough. But the kind of thing represented by Joan Grant, or the 'Seer of Brahan', Kenneth Odhar, involves so many problems with such fundamental concepts as time, free will, the nature of physical matter, and more besides, that any attempt to unravel the implications leaves the mind reeling not least because there seems nothing certain in the Universe if these things are true.

So it is not surprising that orthodox scientists have found it difficult to take claims for the paranormal seriously. Not only does it undermine everything they believe they have demonstrated about the nature of reality, it is simply terrifying as well. And that in turn tells us a lot about why research into the paranormal is so scarce – and why what little is done comes in for such violent attack.

Not that sometimes scientists don't have a point. Even if on those occasions it doesn't take a person with rigorous scientific training to see the flaws in the case. An instance that springs to mind is Uri Geller's remarkable claim that his powers were in the gift of some form of extra-terrestrial entities. Just why Geller should be singled out for special treatment when so many others with similar abilities were not, was not at all clear. Even supposing we accept in the first place that extra-terrestrials are hovering near our planet, ready to take a helping or hindering hand in our affairs such extravagant ideas do not help the cause of serious research into the paranormal, and they may not have been entirely Geller's own. Quite what the place of Andrej Puharich was in this affair has never been made clear, though it would seem that, even if by accident, Puharich attracts odd events and unusual behaviour. And even if Puharich is in some way a focus *himself* for paranormal events, Geller's metal-bending abilities seem real enough – and have not been explained to anyone's satisfaction, by scientists or anyone else.

Finally, there are three people in this collection whose talents were not strictly speaking paranormal, but whose activities most certainly remain unexplained. They are the Count St Germain, who appears to have wandered around Europe for many more years than one man's natural lifespan; the alchemist Fulcanelli, who seems to have discovered the art of turning base metal into gold – and if he did not, then certainly he discovered something very strange, something that had the strangest effects on him; and the necromancer John Dee who, despite almost certainly being duped by his assistant, nonetheless concocted a form of ritual magic that actually seems to work for its practitioners. Like those with paranormal capacities, these men seem to have tapped some force, power or aspect of the Universe that most people scarcely imagine, let alone glimpse; though it manifested itself in a manner quite different from the other strange talents discussed in this volume.

Perhaps one day we will know what it is that allows such people to act in the way that they do – maybe then we will all be able to develop our own strange talents. After all, every one of us has some musical potential – and can be trained to improve it. Why shouldn't the same be true, given the right way to go about it, of the paranormal?

PETER BROOKESMITH

The self-styled Count St Germain – alchemist, diplomat and adventurer – led a chequered career in the royal courts of 18th-century Europe. Some believe the enigmatic Count is still alive; FRANK SMYTH explores the myths

The man from nowhere

TOWARDS THE END of the year 1745 London was gripped by 'spy fever'. It was the year in which the Young Pretender, Prince Charles Edward Stuart, had staged his Jacobite rebellion in an attempt to regain the British throne for his father. Although the Jacobite cause had been defeated at the battle of Culloden in April, it was feared that Jacobite plotters and their French sympathisers might be in hiding in London. Foreigners, particularly Frenchmen, were prime suspects. One such man was arrested in November and accused of having pro-Stuart letters in his possession. He indignantly claimed that the correspondence had been 'planted' on him and, somewhat surprisingly, he was believed and released.

Commenting on the case in a letter to Sir Horace Mann, dated 9 December, Horace Walpole wrote:

> The other day they seized an odd man who goes by the name of Count Saint-Germain. He has been here these two years, and will not tell who he is or whence, but professes that he does not go by his right name. He sings and plays on the violin wonderfully, is mad and not very sensible.

Walpole's comment sheds a tantalising and authentic light on one of the strangest characters of 18th-century high society – a man described by Count Warnstedt as 'the completest charlatan, fool, rattle-pate, windbag and swindler', and by his last patron, Prince Charles of Hesse-Cassel, as 'perhaps one of the greatest sages who ever lived. . . .'

Dazzle of diamonds

The first of the scant historical records of Count St Germain dates from about 1740, when he began to move in fashionable Viennese circles, a handsome man who appeared to be in his thirties. His clothes attracted attention in those days of brightly coloured silks and satins, for he habitually wore black, relieved only by crisp white linen at neck and wrists. The sombreness of his clothes, however, was brilliantly set off by a dazzle of diamonds on his fingers, his fob, his snuff box and his shoe buckles; according to later accounts he also carried handfuls of loose diamonds in his pockets in lieu of money.

In Vienna he met Counts Zabor and Lobkowitz, contemporary leaders of fashion, and through them the ailing French Marshal de Belle Isle, who had been taken seriously ill while campaigning in Germany. The nature of his illness is not recorded, but according to the Marshal it was Count St Germain who

Left: the only known portrait of the man who called himself the Count St Germain, an engraving made for the Marquise d'Urfé in 1783, when the Count must have been in his late sixties, and shortly before his reported death. St Germain was arrested in London as a spy some months after the defeat of the Scottish forces at Culloden in 1745 (below). He was accused of carrying letters for the Young Pretender, Charles Edward Stuart (below left), but was soon released. He then returned to Paris, where he was introduced to Louis XV by Jeanne Antoinette de Pompadour, the king's mistress (right). Sent to the Hague by Louis, St Germain lost the friendship of Giacomo Casanova (below right), who has left us some of the most revealing descriptions of the Count

cured it, and in gratitude he took him to France and set him up with apartments and a well-equipped laboratory.

The bare bones of the Count's life after his arrival in Paris are well documented, but it is the long-vanished detail that provides the lasting mystery.

The legend begins shortly after the Count's arrival in Paris. One evening, according to the pseudonymous 'Countess de B. . .' in her memoirs, *Chroniques de l'oeil de boeuf*, the Count had attended a soirée given by the aged Countess von Georgy, whose late husband had been Ambassador to Venice in the 1670s. Hearing the Count announced, the Countess said she recalled the name from her days in Venice. Had the Count's father perhaps been there at that time? No, replied the Count, but *he* had been, and well remembered the Countess as a beautiful young girl. Impossible, replied the Countess. The man she had known then was 45 at least, roughly the same age as he himself was now.

'Madame,' said the Count, smiling. 'I am very old.'

'But then you must be nearly 100 years old,' exclaimed the Countess.

'That is not impossible,' the Count replied and recounted some details that convinced the Countess, who exclaimed: 'I am already convinced. You are a most extraordinary man, a devil.'

'For pity's sake!' exclaimed the Count in a thundering voice. 'No such names!' He appeared to be seized with a cramp-like trembling in every limb, and left the room immediately.

Many such stories circulated – and were believed – in fashionable French circles during the days of the Count's early fame. He hinted, for instance, that he had known the Holy Family intimately, had been present at the marriage feast at Cana, and had 'always

known that Christ would meet a bad end.' He had been particularly fond of Anne, the mother of the Virgin Mary, and had personally proposed her canonisation at the Council of Nicaea in AD 325.

In Paris the Count soon charmed the jaded Louis XV and his mistress, Madame de Pompadour. The truth about his two-year stay in England before his arrest in 1745 may never be known, but he could well have been engaged on a secret mission; on his return to France he carried out several delicate political errands for the King.

In 1760 Louis sent Count St Germain to the Hague as his own personal representative, ostensibly to arrange a loan with Austria to help finance the Seven Years' War against England. While in Holland, the Count fell out with his erstwhile friend Casanova, also a diplomat at the Hague, who tried hard but unsuccessfully to discredit him in public. But St Germain also made a more powerful enemy. The Duc de Choiseul, Louis's Foreign Minister, discovered that the Count had been putting out feelers with a view to arranging peace between England and France. Somehow the Duke convinced Louis that Count St Germain had betrayed him, and the Count was forced to flee, first back to England and then to Holland.

For two or three years he lived in Holland under the name Count Surmont and set about raising money to build laboratories in which he made paint and dyes and tried to perfect the techniques of alchemy, 'the ennoblement of metals'. He seems to have been successful, for records show that he disappeared from Holland with 100,000 guilders – only to turn up in Belgium, this time calling himself the Marquis de Monferrat. Here, in Tournai, he set up another laboratory before vanishing again.

Over the next few years reports of the

Count's activities continued to come from various parts of Europe. In 1768 he appeared in Russia at the court of Catherine the Great. Turkey had just declared war on Russia, and it seems that his powers as a diplomat and as an insider in French politics stood him in good stead, for before long he was advising Count Alexei Orlov, head of the Russian Imperial Forces. As a reward he was made a high-ranking officer in the Russian Army, this time choosing an ironic English alias – General Welldone. At this point he could have settled down in Russia to lead an honoured and profitable life, but after the defeat of the Turks at the battle of Chesmé in 1770 he chose to go travelling again.

In 1774 he turned up in Nuremberg, seeking funds from Charles Alexander, Margrave of Brandenburg, to set up another laboratory. This time he claimed to be Prince Rákóczy, one of three brothers from Transylvania. At first the Margrave was impressed, particularly when Count Orlov visited Nuremberg on a state visit and embraced the

were lame. The Prince declared he was not a Mason, while the Count feebly replied that he was, but had forgotten all the secret signs.

In 1779 Count St Germain came to his last known resting place, at Eckenförde in Schleswig, Germany. He was an old man, probably in his late sixties, although typically he claimed to be much older. Some of his surface charm had gone, and at first he failed to make much impression on Prince Charles of Hesse-Cassel – but soon, like his predecessors, the Prince was won over.

By this time St Germain, who by all accounts had previously paid at least lip service to the Catholic Church, was openly mystical in his thinking. He told Prince Charles:

Be the torch of the world. If your light is that only of a planet, you will be as nothing in the sight of God. I reserve for you a splendour, of which the solar glory is a shadow. You shall guide the course of the stars, and those who rule Empires shall be guided by you.

Parish records show that on 27 February 1784 Count St Germain died at Prince Charles's home on Eckenförde. He was buried locally, and his last patron erected a tombstone bearing the words:

He who called himself the Comte de Saint-Germain and Welldone of whom there is no other information, has been buried in this church.

But was the Count dead? There is evidence that he appeared to a number of people over the years from 1784 to 1820; some occultists believe he is still alive. The mystery has lived on and deepened in the two centuries since his supposed death.

Following his exile from France, Count St Germain went to the court of Catherine the Great of Russia (top), where he soon achieved high standing as a diplomat and took the title of 'General Welldone'. Towards the end of his career he began to claim that he was a high-ranking Freemason. The illustration (above) shows the ceremony of the entered Apprentice, the first degree of masonry, in the 'Scottish' rite, in a Paris lodge during the 1740s. Laid on the floor is a 'tracing board', used to instruct the new member in the symbolism of masonry

Right: Prince Charles of Hesse-Cassel, the Count's last patron, in whose castle he died

'Prince' warmly. But on checking, the Margrave found that all three Rákóczys were indubitably dead, and that the 'Prince' was in fact Count St Germain. The Count made no attempt to deny these charges, but felt it prudent to move on, and did so in 1776.

The Duc de Choiseul claimed that St Germain had worked as a double agent for Frederick the Great during his period at the French court. If this were so, his old master preferred to forget the connection, for a letter from Count St Germain to Frederick begging for patronage was ignored. Undaunted, the Count went to Leipzig and presented himself before Prince Frederick Augustus of Brunswick, claiming to be a Freemason of the fourth grade.

This was a bold move, for Frederick Augustus was Grand Master of the Prussian Masonic Lodges – and, unaccountably, it was a move that went wrong. If he was a confidence trickster, Count St Germain in his prime had few equals at the game; his background stories generally stood up to close scrutiny. This time, however, they

Searching for St Germain

Fluent linguist, 'wonderful' musician and painter, gifted jeweller, healer – the talents of the Count St Germain seemed endless. FRANK SMYTH concludes his account of the adventurer's remarkable career

Above: '. . . intended by nature to be the king of impostors', as Casanova described him, Count St Germain claimed to know all the secrets of alchemy, including the nature of the Elixir of Life. He set up numerous laboratories in different countries in Europe; they would have looked very like this alchemist's laboratory portrayed by Pietro Longhi

THE MYSTERY surrounding the Count St Germain is deepened by the genuine uncertainty about his origins, which remains today. One account states that he was born in 1710 in San Germano, the son of a tax collector. Eliphas Levi, the 19th century occultist, claimed that St Germain was born in Lentmeritz in Bohemia, the bastard son of a noble Rosicrucian, at the end of the 17th century. The date fits, and the background would account for the Count's strong leaning towards mysticism as well as his formidable talents – even if they were not 'powers' in the paranormal sense of the word.

He had, for instance, a genuine gift for languages; it is known that he spoke fluent French, German, English, Dutch and Russian, and he claimed that he was also a master of Chinese, Hindu and Persian – although there can have been few people around with sufficient knowledge of these languages to challenge him.

Horace Walpole wrote that the Count was a 'wonderful' musician. He was also a 'wonderful' painter – although none of his canvases are known to have survived. The uniqueness of his oils seems to have lain in the fact that he could reproduce jewels which 'glittered . . . as in the life'.

There is plenty of evidence that St Germain was an expert jeweller – although not, as he claimed, that he had studied the art with the Shah of Persia. He is reported to have delighted Louis XV by repairing a flawed diamond and it may well be that he decorated his famous jewel paintings with mother-of-pearl or some such substance.

He also had an excellent knowledge of chemistry in all its branches; the many laboratories that he set up with borrowed money throughout Europe were all apparently devoted to the production of brighter and better pigments and dyes, as well as to the study of the ennoblement of metals – alchemy.

St Germain also had a reputation as a healer; besides curing the Marshal de Belle Isle, he revived a young friend of Madame de Pompadour after mushroom poisoning had almost killed her.

The Count was reputed never to eat in company – he sat and sipped mineral water

Below: St Germain claimed to have studied the art of jewellery at the court of the Shah of Persia, where he is said to have lived from 1737 to 1742. The many fantastic claims made by the Count, and the persistent stories that he was alive well into the 19th century, caused Napoleon III (below right) to set up a special commission to enquire into the matter. The findings of the commission were, however, completely destroyed in a fire at the Hotel de Ville, Paris, in 1871 (below, far right), an event that the supporters of the Count's story maintained was not an accident

while everyone around him was gorging in the self-indulgent manner of the time. This can only have added to his air of mystery. Casanova was certainly impressed:

> Instead of eating, he talked from the beginning of the meal to the end, and I followed his example in one respect as I did not eat, but listened to him with the greatest attention. It may safely be said that as a conversationalist he was unequalled.

In fact, as Colin Wilson points out in *The occult*, the Count was probably simply a vegetarian.

The real remaining mystery surrounding the legend of St Germain lies in the question of where he gained all his specialised knowledge. Again there is a simple answer: experience. The Count's 19th-century followers insisted that the knowledge was his when he first appeared at the French court in the 1740s, but it is more likely that he amassed it

during his long life; after all, he lived at least into his seventies.

Not all of St Germain's contemporaries were impressed by his talents. Casanova, who met him in the Hague when they were both on diplomatic missions there, regarded him as a charlatan, but nevertheless found him charming:

> This extraordinary man, intended by nature to be the king of impostors and quacks, would say in an easy, assured manner that he was three hundred years old, that he knew the secret of the Universal Medicine, that he possessed a mastery over nature, that he could melt diamonds, professing himself capable of forming, out of 10 or 12 small diamonds, one of the finest water . . . All this, he said, was a mere trifle to him. Notwithstanding his boastings, his bare-faced lies, and his manifold eccentricities, I cannot say I found him offensive. In spite of my knowledge of what he was and in spite of my own feelings, I thought him an astonishing man . . .

And in 1777 Count Alvensleben, Prussian Ambassador to the Court at Dresden, who knew St Germain well, wrote of him:

> He is a highly gifted man with a very alert mind, but completely without judgement, and he has only gained his singular reputation by the lowest and basest flattery of which a man is capable, as well as by his outstanding eloquence, especially if one lets oneself be carried away by the fervour and enthusiasm with which he can express himself. Inordinate vanity is the mainspring driving his whole mechanism.

Many of the stories about St Germain that gave rise to these sceptical attitudes did not actually stem from the Count himself but, as was revealed by the researches of Gustav Berthold Volz in the 1920s, from the mouth of an impostor named Gauve. Gauve was

Left: Louis XVI says farewell to his family, as the gaoler waits to lead him to the guillotine. In her diaries the Queen, Marie Antoinette, regretted that she had not paid heed to St Germain's warnings.

Below left: the famous French singer Emma Calvé autographed this photograph in 1897 to St Germain, 'the great chiromancer, who has told me many truths'.

Below right: Richard Chanfray, a Parisian claiming to be Count St Germain, photographed in 1976

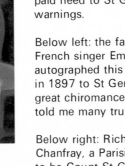

employed by St Germain's arch-enemy, the Duc de Choiseul, who, in his jealousy of the Count, would stop at nothing in his attempts to discredit him. The idea was that Gauve, who looked remarkably like the Count, should wander around society exaggerating the Count's known foibles to discredit him.

Not everyone believes that the Count is dead. Although the parish records at Eckenförde record his death, the legend that he was still alive began almost immediately afterwards. The Count's last patron, Prince Charles of Hesse-Cassel, added to the mystery surrounding his death by burning all his papers 'lest they be misinterpreted', while another of his followers from Hesse broadcast the news that he was not dead, but had appeared in Paris and foretold the outbreak of the French Revolution to Marie Antoinette – who, in her diaries, regretted not having taken note of what he said earlier. He made another appearance, witnessed by many people, at Wilhelmsbad in 1785, a year after his supposed death – accompanied, so it was said, by the magician Cagliostro, the hypnotist Anton Mesmer, and the 'unknown philosopher', Louis Claude de St Martin.

In 1789 he went to Sweden to warn King Gustavus III of danger, and visited his friend, the diarist Mademoiselle d'Adhémar – who noted that he still looked like a man of 46 – and told her that he would see her five times more. She claimed that this did, indeed, happen – 'always to my unspeakable surprise' – the last occasion being the night before the Duc de Berri's murder in 1820.

The legend lives on

The Emperor Napoleon III (1808–1873) was so intrigued by the story that he ordered a special commission to be set up to investigate the life and doings of the enigmatic Count. The commission's findings were destroyed in a disastrous fire that consumed the Hôtel de Ville in Paris in 1871 – an event that the Count's followers found impossible to ascribe to coincidence.

A few years later Madame Blavatsky's Theosophical Society announced that St Germain was one of its 'hidden masters' – immortals whose stores of secret knowledge were available to adepts for the enrichment of the world – along with such figures as Christ, Buddha, Apollonius of Tyana, Christian Rosencreutz and Francis Bacon. It is said that a group of theosophists went to Paris after its liberation from the Nazis, convinced they would meet the Count; apparently he failed to turn up.

Nevertheless, the legend of this enigmatic figure lives on. As recently as January 1972 a Parisian called Richard Chanfray appeared on French television claiming to be the Count St Germain. In front of the TV cameras, using a camping gas stove, he apparently successfully turned lead into gold. Will the Count appear again? Time only deepens the mystery of his true nature.

Croiset: the psychic detective

The Dutch clairvoyant and healer Gerard Croiset was often successful in locating missing persons – dead or alive – and frequently made the headlines for his work with the police. ROY STEMMAN outlines the life and work of this remarkable psychic

EIGHT WEEKS after his 24-year-old daughter Carol had disappeared, Professor Walter E. Sandelius was prepared to try anything to find her. Carol had disappeared from a hospital in Topeka, Kansas, USA, and although photographs of the attractive young woman had been circulated throughout the country she was still missing.

Walter Sandelius, a professor of political science at the University of Kansas, had read about the Dutch clairvoyant and healer Gerard Croiset, who had a reputation for finding missing people – dead or alive – and solving crimes with his psychic powers.

So, on 11 December 1959, with no other immediate hope of finding his daughter, he telephoned Utrecht University. He spoke to Professor Willem Tenhaeff, the parapsychologist who had spent many years studying Croiset, and arranged to call again the following day when the clairvoyant would be in Tenhaeff's office.

When he did so, Croiset told the Kansas professor: 'I see your daughter running over a large lawn and then crossing a viaduct. Now I see her at a place where there are stores, and near them a large body of water with landing stages and many small boats. I see her riding there in a lorry and in a big red car.'

'Is she still alive?' asked the anxious father.

'Yes, don't worry,' said Croiset. 'You will hear something definite at the end of six days.'

On the sixth day, as arranged with Croiset, Professor Sandelius went downstairs at 8 a.m. to telephone Tenhaeff. As he picked up the telephone he glanced towards the living room and was astonished to see his daughter sitting on the sofa! Subsequent questioning of the Dutch clairvoyant proved that he had successfully 'seen' across nearly 5000 miles (8000 kilometres) and described Carol's movements with impressive accuracy.

This is one of hundreds of such cases that were investigated and kept on file at Utrecht University. Many were described in Jackson Harrison Pollack's book, *Croiset, the clairvoyant*. But not all had such happy endings. Croiset was often the first person to break the news to relatives that a missing person was dead. Sadly in many of the cases they were children who had fallen into Holland's waterway system and drowned.

The father of five children, Croiset was

Left: Croiset using an electronic version of the Zener card experiment, designed to test the powers of precognition. Croiset's guesses were often significantly above average

Below: Croiset tells the Dutch police in 1963: 'The body is there – you can look for it.' He had located the body of a missing boy in the Vliet Canal through psychic means alone

always eager to help distraught parents whose sons or daughters had disappeared, and he refused to take any money for his psychic work.

In the case of one missing boy, Wimpje Slee, Croiset told an uncle over the telephone that he had fallen into the water and drowned, and that his body would be found near a bridge. Then, on Friday 19 April 1963, in order to get stronger impressions, he met the boy's uncle and was able to tell him that Wimpje had drowned near a small house with a slanted weather-vane. But, he added, his body was no longer there. It would be found, however, on Tuesday, between two bridges near the house described.

Newspapers in The Hague heard of the story and published Croiset's prediction the following day, enabling their readers to check for themselves. On Tuesday, 23 April – just as Croiset had foretold – Wimpje's body was discovered floating on the Vliet Canal, precisely where the clairvoyant had said it would be found. Not surprisingly, the *Haagsche Courant* headlined its story: 'Croiset proved right once more'.

Pictures of Croiset's craggy features and wiry hair frequently appeared in European and Scandinavian newspapers. He assisted the police to look for missing persons in half a dozen countries and co-operated in tests conducted by leading psychical researchers. But it was to Professor Tenhaeff that he was particularly loyal.

A star performer

Of the 47 psychics and sensitives tested by the professor, Croiset was undoubtedly the star performer. Unlike other clairvoyants who shun research work, Croiset moved to Utrecht in 1956 in order to be closer to the university and to make himself more readily available. And when grateful individuals offered him money for helping to find lost friends or relatives he always declined, saying the only 'reward' he wanted was for them to file a report of what happened with Professor Tenhaeff. As a result, the Utrecht archives must contain some of the best authenticated accounts of clairvoyance on record.

Despite the research work, however, Croiset never really knew how his psychic power functioned. He once described it as like seeing a fine powder, which formed first into dots and then lines. Out of these lines shapes and scenes would form, first in two dimensions then in three. Usually his clairvoyance was in black and white, but if a corpse was involved he would see pictures in colour.

Croiset's involvement in police investigations tends to make his popular image a distorted one. Although he was undoubtedly a brilliant psychic detective, he was hesitant about working on certain cases of murder and theft for fear that he would wrong an innocent person. For example, at the site of a murder he might describe a person in great

Professor Tenhaeff of Utrecht University and the Utrecht Chief of Police are pictured here with Gerard Croiset. They were a regular team, Croiset helping the police in their search for missing persons and Professor Tenhaeff monitoring the clairvoyant's progress. Few psychics have been as rigorously tested as Croiset

detail who was not the murderer, but an innocent passer-by. In fact, Croiset said that in 90 per cent of criminal cases he found it difficult to discover the culprit, though he was able to give police valuable clues. On the other hand, in cases of accidental disappearances it is claimed that Croiset had an 80 per cent success rate.

But it was not necessary for Croiset to wait for crimes to be committed or for people to vanish in order to prove that he possessed extra-sensory powers. Instead, Professor Tenhaeff devised a 'chair test', which was repeated with astonishing accuracy over 20 years or more. It demonstrated that Croiset could apparently see into the near future.

It worked like this: a week or more in advance of a large public meeting, Croiset would be asked to make written statements about the person who would sit in a specific seat. On the day of the meeting, individuals would be allowed to sit where they wanted (no one knowing which chair had been selected) or were given numbered tickets at random as they arrived directing them to sit in certain seats. Then Croiset's predictions would be read to the audience. Time and again, the unsuspecting person sitting in the pre-selected seat confirmed that the majority of the statements Croiset had made were correct. These would often consist of the person's sex, a physical description and details of their work, people around them, or descriptions of specific incidents in their life. Occasionally, Croiset could get no advance impressions – in which case it was usually discovered that the seat was left unoccupied on the night.

Gerard Croiset died on 20 July 1980, at the age of 71. But the records on file at Utrecht University of the world's most tested psychic will continue to intrigue and baffle scientists for many years to come.

Tom Lethbridge

Tom Lethbridge is a major figure in the world of the paranormal, but, as COLIN WILSON explains, he took many years of painstaking academic and practical research to reach his important conclusions

NO ONE WHO IS interested in the paranormal can afford to ignore Tom Lethbridge, yet when he died in a nursing home in Devon in 1971, his name was hardly known to the general public. Today, many of his admirers believe that he is the single most important name in the history of psychical research. His ideas on dowsing, life after death, ghosts, poltergeists, magic, second-sight, precognition, the nature of time, cover a wider field than those of any other psychical researcher. Moreover, they fit together into the most exciting and comprehensive theory of the 'occult' ever advanced.

These ideas were expressed in a series of small books published in the last 10 years of his life. The odd thing is that Lethbridge took no interest in psychic matters until he retired to Devon in his mid fifties. He was trained as an archaeologist and a historian, and spent most of his adult life in Cambridge as the Keeper of Anglo-Saxon Antiquities at the University Museum. But even in that respectable setting he was a maverick, and in 1957 he left Cambridge in disgust at the

Above: Tom and Mina Lethbridge were keen – and accomplished – dowsers

Below: Ladram Bay, Devon, where people felt a strong urge to jump off the cliffs

hostile reception of one of his books on archaeology. Together with his wife Mina, he moved into Hole House, an old Tudor mansion on the south coast of Devon. He meant to spend his retirement reading and digging for bits of broken pottery. In fact, the most amazing period of his eventful life was about to begin.

The person who was most responsible for this change of direction was an old 'witch' who lived next door. This white haired little old lady assured Lethbridge that she could put mild spells on people who annoyed her, and that she was able to leave her body at night and wander around the district – an ability known as 'astral projection'. Lethbridge was naturally sceptical – until something convinced him.

The witch explained to him one day how she managed to put off unwanted visitors. What she did was to draw a five pointed star – a pentagram – in her head, and then visualise it across the path of the unwanted visitor – for example, on the front gate.

Shortly afterwards, Tom was lying in bed, idly drawing pentagrams in his head, and imagining them around their beds. In the middle of the night, Mina woke up with a creepy feeling that there was somebody else in the room. At the foot of the bed, she could see a faint glow of light, which slowly faded

A seeker after truth

as she watched it. The next day, the witch came to see them. When she told them that she had 'visited' their bedroom on the previous night, and found the beds surrounded by triangles of fire, Tom's scepticism began to evaporate. Mina politely requested the old witch to stay out of their bedroom at night.

Three years later, the old lady died in peculiar circumstances. She was quarrelling with a neighbouring farmer, and told Lethbridge that she intended to put a spell on the man's cattle. By this time, Lethbridge knew enough about the 'occult' to take her seriously, and he warned her about the dangers of black magic – how it could rebound on to the witch. But the old lady ignored his advice. One morning, she was found dead in her bed in circumstances that made the police suspect murder. And the cattle of two nearby farms suddenly got foot and mouth disease. However, the farmer she wanted to 'ill wish' remained unaffected. Lethbridge was convinced that the spell had gone wrong and 'bounced back'.

The invisible world

But the old lady's death resulted – indirectly – in one of his most important insights. Passing the witch's cottage, he experienced a 'nasty feeling', a suffocating sense of depression. With a scientist's curiosity, he walked around the cottage, and noticed an interesting thing. He could step *into* the depression and then out of it again, just as if it was some kind of invisible wall.

The depression reminded Lethbridge of something that had happened when he was a teenager. He and his mother had gone for a walk in the Great Wood near Wokingham. It was a lovely morning; yet quite suddenly, both of them experienced 'a horrible feeling of gloom and depression, which crept upon us like a blanket of fog over the surface of the sea'. They hurried away, agreeing that it was something terrible and inexplicable. A few days later, the corpse of a suicide was found a few yards from the spot where they had been standing, hidden by some bushes.

About a year after the death of the witch, another strange experience gave Tom the clue he was looking for. On a damp January afternoon, he and Mina drove down to Ladram Bay to collect seaweed for her garden. As Lethbridge stepped on to the beach, he once again experienced the feeling of gloom and fear, like a blanket of fog descending upon him. Mina wandered off along the beach while Tom filled the sacks with seaweed. Suddenly she came hurrying back, saying: 'Let's go. I can't stand this place a minute longer. There's something frightful here.'

The next day, they mentioned what had happened to Mina's brother. He said he also had experienced the same kind of thing in a field near Avebury, in Wiltshire. The word 'field' made something connect in Tom's brain – he remembered that field telephones

Above: Hole Mill and Hole House in Devon. Hole Mill was the home of Lethbridge's neighbour, a 'witch' or 'wise woman' whose strange powers convinced Lethbridge that the world of the paranormal was worth investigating. Hole House became the Lethbridges' home after Tom left Cambridge in disgust at the reception of one of his books. Here he was to develop his theories on psychic phenomena until his death in 1971

often short-circuit in warm, muggy weather. 'What was the weather like?' he asked. 'Warm and damp,' said the brother.

An idea was taking shape. *Water . . .* could that be the key? It had been warm and damp in the Great Wood. It had been warm and damp on Ladram beach. The following weekend, they set out for Ladram Bay a second time. Again, as they stepped on to the beach, both walked into the same bank of depression – or 'ghoul' as Lethbridge called it. Mina led Tom to the far end of the beach, to the place she had been sitting when she had been overwhelmed by the strange feeling. Here it was so strong that it made them feel giddy – Lethbridge described it as the feeling you get when you have a high temperature and are full of drugs. On either side of them were two small streams.

Mina wandered off to look at the scenery from the top of the cliff. Suddenly, she walked into the depression again. Moreover, she had an odd feeling, as if someone – or something – was urging her to jump over. She went and fetched Tom, who agreed that the spot was just as sinister as the place down on the seashore below.

Now he needed only one more piece of the jigsaw puzzle, and he found it – but only years later. Nine years after the first known experiences of depression were felt on those cliffs a man did commit suicide there. Lethbridge wondered whether the 'ghoul' was a feeling so intense that it had become timeless and imprinted itself on the area, casting its baleful shadow on those who stood there.

Whether from the past or from the future the feelings of despair were 'recorded' on the surroundings – but how?

The key, Lethbridge believed, was water. As an archaeologist, he had always been mildly interested in dowsing and water-divining. The dowser walks along with a forked hazel twig held in his hands, and when he stands above running water, the muscles in his hands and arms convulse and the twig bends either up or down. How does it work? Professor Y. Rocard of the Sorbonne discovered that underground water produces changes in the earth's magnetic field, and this is what the dowser's muscles respond to. The water does this because it has a field of its own, which interacts with the earth's field.

Significantly, magnetic fields are the means by which sound is recorded on tape covered with iron oxide. Suppose the magnetic field of running water can also record strong emotions – which, after all, are basically electrical activities in the human brain and body? Such fields could well be strongest in damp and muggy weather.

Magnetic emotions

This would also explain why the banks of depression seem to form a kind of invisible wall. Anyone who has ever tried bringing a magnet closer and closer to an iron nail will know that the nail is suddenly 'seized' by the magnet as it enters the force field. Presumably the magnetic field of water has the same property. And if it can 'tape record' powerful emotions, then you would feel them quite suddenly, as you stepped into the field. Both Tom and Mina noticed that the ghoul on Ladram beach came to an end quite abruptly

And what about 'ghosts' – that is, things actually seen, rather than just sensed? Here again, Lethbridge was convinced that his electrical theory fitted the facts. In 1922 – when he was an undergraduate at Cambridge – he had seen a ghost in the rooms of a friend. He was just about to leave, late at night, when the door opened and a man wearing a top hat came in. Assuming he was a college porter who had come to give his friend a message, Lethbridge said goodnight, and went out. The man did not reply. The next morning, Lethbridge saw his friend, and asked casually about the identity of the man in the top hat. His friend flatly denied that anyone had come in. And when Lethbridge brooded on it, he realised that the man had not worn a porter's uniform. He wore hunting kit. Then why had he not recognised the red coat? Because it wasn't red; it was grey – a dull grey, like a black and white *photograph*. Lethbridge realised that he had seen a ghost. Moreover, his friend's rooms overlooked the river, so there was a damp atmosphere.

Tom had seen a ghost in the witch's garden, in the year before she died. He had been sitting on the hillside, looking down at the witch's house, when he noticed two women in the yard. One was the witch; the other was a tall old lady dressed in rather old-fashioned grey clothes. Later, he saw the witch and asked her about her visitor. The witch looked puzzled; then, when Lethbridge described the figure, said, 'Ah, you've seen my ghost.'

This happened in 1959, before Lethbridge had his important insight on Ladram beach. So it never entered his head that the ghost was a 'tape recording'. His first

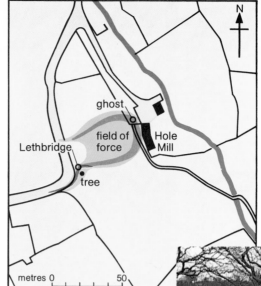

Left: map showing the position of the ghost at Hole Mill in relation to the underground stream and its field of force. Lethbridge plotted the area 'blind' with his hazel twig. Later excavation showed this plot to be correct in every detail

Right: the 'witch's' house, Hole Mill, as seen from Hole House. This was the spot where Lethbridge saw the ghost of an old lady and experienced a curious tingling sensation when he stood over an underground stream. He later discovered that the two experiences were connected

Below: the Reverend Bishop Leonidas Polk, who intrigued Professor Joseph Buchanan in the 1840s by being able to detect brass in the dark simply by touching it with his fingers

thought was that the old lady in grey might be some kind of thought projection – in other words, a kind of television picture, caused by someone else *thinking* about the ghost, and somehow transferring the thought into his own mind. Then it struck him that ghosts are supposed to reappear on anniversaries. So he and Mina decided they would go to the same spot at the same time the following year, and see what happened.

In fact, nothing happened. They stood quietly at the same spot, on a fine, warm morning, but the old lady failed to reappear. However, both of them noticed a kind of electrical tingling feeling in the atmosphere. There was a tiny underground stream running down the lane – under a drain cover – and they felt the tingling most strongly when they stood on top of it. Tom would only realise the significance of that tingling feeling after his experience on Ladram beach. And then he decided to explore the stream and see where it led. The result confirmed his suspicions. The stream turned at right angles quite close to the witch's house. And it was directly above this stream that he had seen the old lady in grey. He had been connected to the spot by the magnetic field of the flowing water. But the witch, standing a few yards away from the underground stream, had seen nothing.

So Lethbridge had been quite mistaken to believe that his 'old lady' was some kind of television picture projected by someone else's mind, or a ghost that would return exactly a year later. It was almost certainly just another 'tape recording' – a kind of videotape recording this time – but in black and white, just like the huntsman he had seen in his friend's rooms at Cambridge.

It would be very satisfying to be able to add that he decided to investigate the apparitions, and found that a huntsman had died of apoplexy in the room in Cambridge, or that the old lady had drowned in the underground stream. No such neat, satisfactory solutions can be provided. And neither is it necessary. The huntsman had probably been a previous inhabitant of the rooms; the old lady had probably lived most of her life in Hole Mill – the witch's house. (From her clothes, Lethbridge thought she dated back to before the First World War.) But there is no earthly reason why the 'force field' of water should record only unpleasant emotions. The old lady might have been unusually happy or excited when she was 'photographed' on the field. Or perhaps she passed over the spot so often that her image finally became indelibly imprinted there.

How much evidence is there for the Lethbridge theory of ghosts and ghouls? Well, to begin with, it is worth noting that his 'tape recording' theory was by no means new. In America in the 1840s, a professor named Joseph Rhodes Buchanan was intrigued when a certain Bishop Polk told him that he could

A diagram showing the 'psyche-field' around a tree, plotted with a hazel twig. The shaded area shows the limits of the force field that can be 'picked up' by a dowser

A Hawaiian volcano erupting. In the mid 19th century William Denton gave a piece of volcanic rock to a sensitive who 'saw' a volcano exploding. This was one of the first serious experiments into psychometry – or object reading – and its results had far-reaching implications for dowsing

detect brass in the dark by touching it with his fingers; it produced an unpleasant taste in his mouth. Buchanan tested him and found it was true. He discovered that certain of his students also had the same curious ability. In fact, some of them could even detect different substances when they were wrapped up in brown paper. Buchanan decided that the nerves produce some kind of force field – he called it the 'nerve aura' – which streams out of the finger ends, and which operates like an extra sense.

A strange talent

What really puzzled him was that some of his sensitives could hold a sealed letter, and describe the person who had written it, and whether the writer was sad or happy at the time. Buchanan explained this by suggesting that all substances give off emanations (another name for a force field) on which human emotions can be recorded. He had stumbled on Lethbridge's theory just about 100 years before Lethbridge.

Buchanan's friend William Denton, a professor of geology, took the theory even further. He tried wrapping a piece of Hawaiian volcanic rock in paper and handing it to a sensitive, who immediately saw in his mind an island in the midst of blue seas, and an exploding volcano. When handed a pebble of glacial limestone, the sensitive saw it frozen in deep ice. A fragment of meteor produced a picture of the depths of space, with glittering stars. Denton was so excited by all this that he believed he had discovered a new – or forgotten – human faculty, and that one day we shall be able to look back into the past just as easily as we can now look at the stars (which may have died millions of years ago) through a telescope.

Buchanan and Denton called this strange faculty *psychometry*, and for a few years it caused considerable excitement in the scientific world. Then, with the coming of Darwin, T. H. Huxley and the rest, a more sceptical climate prevailed, and it was forgotten. Even so, Sir Oliver Lodge, the notable scientist who dared to be interested in psychical research, wrote in 1908:

> Take, for example, a haunted house . . . wherein some one room is the scene of a ghostly representation of some long past tragedy. On a psychometric hypothesis, the original tragedy has been literally *photographed* on its material surroundings, nay, even on the ether itself, by reason of the intensity of emotion felt by those who enacted it.

It may seem, then, that Lethbridge's discovery was not so remarkable after all. That would be a mistake. For it was only a part of a far more comprehensive and more important theory of the paranormal.

The master dowser

During his career as an archaeologist Tom Lethbridge discovered dowsing – 'picking up' electrical fields of objects and reacting to them. But this fascinating ability was only the beginning of an important series of experiments

ALTHOUGH TOM LETHBRIDGE had no interest in ghosts or 'ghouls' before he retired to Devon, he had always been fascinated by dowsing.

It all started in the early 1930s, when he and another archaeologist were looking for Viking graves on the island of Lundy in the Bristol Channel. They located the graves, then, having time on their hands while they waited for the boat back to the mainland, they decided to try some experiments with dowsing. Hidden under the soil of Lundy Island are seams of volcanic rock that pass up through the slate. Lethbridge decided to see if he could locate these. So he cut himself a hazel twig, allowed his friend to blindfold him, and was then led along the cliff path, the forked hazel twig held tightly in his hands. (The twig has to be held with the forks bent slightly apart, so it has a certain amount of 'spring'.) Every time he passed over a volcanic seam, the hazel fork twisted violently in his hands. His friend had an extra-sensitive

Above: Tom Lethbridge, the archaeologist who became a master dowser

Top: the island of Lundy in the Bristol Channel, where Lethbridge conducted his first experiment into dowsing. Using a forked hazel twig, he and a colleague dowsed for volcanic seams. The hazel twig located the seams by twisting violently when held over them

magnetometer, so he was able to verify that Lethbridge had accurately located every single one of the volcanic seams.

To Lethbridge, that seemed logical enough. Like running water, a volcanic seam has a faint magnetic field. Presumably he was somehow able to pick up these fields through the hazel twig, which reacted like a sensitive instrument. In one of his earlier books he wrote: 'Most people can dowse, if they know how to do it. If they cannot do it, there is probably some fault in the electrical system of their bodies.'

The garden of Lethbridge's house in Devon was full of interesting archaeological remains – some of them dating to Roman times. And, soon after moving in, Lethbridge remembered an experiment he had seen performed in the University Museum of Archaeology and Ethnology in Cambridge. Someone had asserted that a pendulum can tell whether a skull is male or female, and demonstrated this by dangling one over an ancient skull. The pendulum swung back and forth, which meant – apparently – that it was a man's skull. If it had swung round in a circle, the skull would have been female. Midwives sometimes use the same method to determine the sex of an unborn baby, dangling a wedding ring on a piece of thread over the stomach of the pregnant woman.

But how can such a method possibly work? It sounds completely absurd. Male and female skulls do not have electrical fields; and even if they did, there is no reason why one of them should make a pendulum swing back and forth, and the other make it swing in a circle.

With characteristic thoroughness, Lethbridge set out to test it for himself. His first question was: if a pendulum can somehow respond to different substances, then how does it do it? A pendulum is, after all, just a weight fixed to the end of a piece of string. It must be the unconscious mind – or possibly the muscles – of the dowser that respond. But respond to what? The answer seemed to be: to some kind of vibration. In which case, it seems a fair assumption that different lengths of the pendulum respond to different vibrations.

It was the most fruitful assumption he ever made. And he set out to test it by putting a wooden bob on the end of a long piece of string, and then winding the string round a

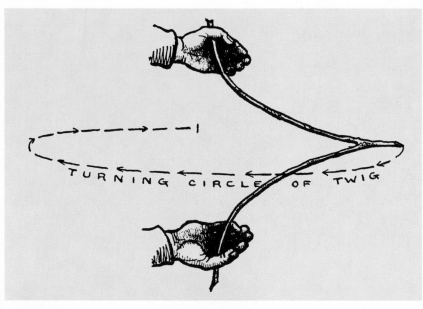

pencil, so he could lengthen or shorten the pendulum at will. Next, he put a piece of silver on the ground, held the pendulum over it, and then carefully began to lengthen the string. And, when he had unwound about 2 feet (60 centimetres), the pendulum suddenly began to go into a circular swing. Lethbridge measured his string. It was precisely 22 inches. (Lethbridge believed one could dowse successfully only using Imperial measurements. Feet and inches, he said, were 'natural' measurements based on the human body, whereas metric measurements were 'unnatural'. So pendulum 'rates' will be given in inches only.)

The pendulum reacts

Next, he went out into the courtyard of Hole House – which dates back to Tudor times – and walked around with his pendulum. At one place, it went into a circular swing. Lethbridge dug down carefully, and eventually located a small piece of Rhineland stoneware pottery. He tried his pendulum over it; it went into a powerful circular swing. That puzzled him greatly, until he tried his 22-inch pendulum over a piece of lead, and it also went into a circular swing. Apparently, 22 inches is the 'rate' for both silver and lead. And Rhineland pottery in the 17th century was glazed with lead.

Now very excited, Lethbridge kept the pendulum at the same length and walked round the courtyard until it went again into a circular swing. He dug down, and found a bit of lead from an Elizabethan window. So he proved that the pendulum was accurate. He tried holding the pendulum over a copper pot, and found that it reacted at $30\frac{1}{2}$ inches. He walked around the courtyard until the pendulum responded, and this time, dug up a tiny copper tube. It was very small, so evidently the pendulum was extremely sensitive.

Convinced that he had made a major discovery, Lethbridge spent days testing all kinds of different substances with his pendulum and discovered, to his delight, that every one of them had its own 'rate': glass, sulphur, iron, slate, amber – even alcohol, garlic and apples. When he held it over a bottle of Australian Burgundy, the pendulum responded at 14, 20, $25\frac{1}{2}$ and 32 inches, which Lethbridge proved to be the 'rates' for glass, vegetable matter (the label), alcohol and iron.

He even tested a truffle – that delicious fungus that is used in *foie gras*. The pendulum responded at 17 inches. Trying to locate any buried truffles, Lethbridge stood with his pendulum in one hand, while pointing his other hand around in a slow semicircle. When the 17-inch pendulum began to swing, he drew a straight line in the direction he was pointing. Then he went and stood several yards away, and repeated the experiment. Where the two lines crossed, he dug down with a trowel. He located a tiny, dark

Above: the characteristic movement of a forked hazel twig when actively dowsing. Its usual – though not invariable – reaction when held over a subterranean stream, for example, is to turn in a circle from right to left

Left: the late S. J. Searles of North Cray, Kent, showing the power of the hazel twig as it pulls downwards when reacting to the presence of underground water

object, the size of a pea, and sent it to the Science Museum in London for identification. Incredibly, it turned out to be a rare variety of truffle.

There were still a number of minor mysteries – such as how to distinguish between lead and silver, when both react at 22 inches, or between truffles and beech wood, both of which respond to a 17-inch pendulum. Further experimentation solved that one. The number of times the pendulum gyrated was equally important. For lead, it gyrates 16 times, then goes back to its normal back-and-forth motion; for silver it gyrates 22 times. It looked as if nature had devised a simple and

Above: the corner of the courtyard at the Lethbridge home, Hole House in Devon, where dowsing revealed a number of buried objects

Below: how dowsing with a pendulum works
A. dowser's psyche-field
B. static field of object
C. pendulum – where A meets B it begins to move in a circle
D. how the pendulum length is controlled by dowser

foolproof code for identifying any substance.

And not just substances. The pendulum also responded to colours – the natural colours of flowers, for example: 22 inches for grey, 29 for yellow, 30 for green, and so on. Lethbridge found himself wondering whether the pendulum would respond to thoughts and emotions as well as substances. A simple, two-part experiment convinced him that this was so. During his last excavations near Cambridge, Lethbridge had collected a number of sling-stones from an Iron Age fort. He tried his pendulum over them, and found that they reacted at 24 inches and also at 40. He fetched a bucketful of stones from the beach and tried the pendulum over those. They failed to react at either 'rate'. Now he divided the stones into two piles, and told his wife Mina to throw half of them at a wall, while he threw the rest. He tried the pendulum again. All Mina's stones now reacted at 29 inches (the 'rate' for females), while those he had thrown reacted at 24 – like the Iron Age stones. So it looked as if the Iron Age stones had been thrown by males. But what about their reaction to a 40-inch pendulum? Could it, he wondered, be the rate for anger or death? Lethbridge set the pendulum at 40 inches and thought about something that made him angry; immediately, the pendulum began to gyrate. So it looked as if 40 was indeed the rate for anger. He later ascertained that it was also the rate for death, cold and blackness.

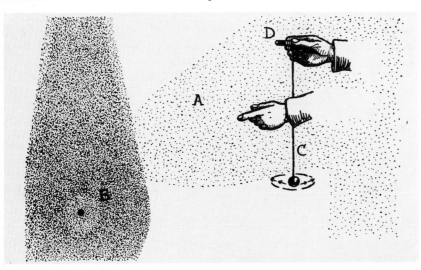

Now all this, admittedly, seems absurd. Yet Lethbridge repeated the experiments dozen of times, and each time he got the same result. The pendulum responded to ideas – like evolution, pride, life, danger and deceit – just as readily as to substances. Moreover Mina got the same results. And, through his experience of psychometry, Lethbridge realised that there is nothing very odd in a pendulum responding to ideas. If a 'sensitive' can hold an unopened letter, and somehow feel the emotions of the person who wrote it, then it seems reasonable to assume that human beings possess some 'sense' that registers these things just as our eyes register colours and shapes – a sixth sense perhaps? In fact, you could say that a pendulum is merely an aid to psychometry. A psychometrist – or sensitive – can pick up these vibrations directly; non-sensitive people, like Lethbridge, can only feel them indirectly through the pendulum.

After months of experiment with the pendulum, Lethbridge constructed tables of the various 'rates'; and it became clear that 40 inches was some kind of limit. Every single substance that he tested fell between zero and 40 inches. And at this point he discovered something rather odd. Sulphur reacts to a 7-inch pendulum. If he extended the pendulum to 47 inches – 40 plus 7 – it would still react to a heap of sulphur. But not when directly over the heap. It only reacted a little

to one side. The same was true of everything else he tried beyond 40 – the pendulum reacted, but a little to one side.

Forty inches is also the 'rate' for death. Was it possible, Lethbridge wondered, that when the pendulum registers beyond 40 inches, it registers a world beyond death – another dimension? He remembered an experience of being at the dentist, under anaesthetic, and finding himself outside his body – hovering up in the air, and slightly to the left – just like the 'displacement' reaction of the pendulum to the heap of sulphur.

He noticed another odd thing. Below 40 inches, there is no 'rate' for the concept of time; the pendulum simply will not respond. But when he lengthened the pendulum to 60 inches, he got a strong reaction for time. He

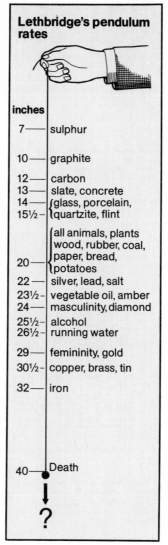

Lethbridge's pendulum rates

inches	
7	sulphur
10	graphite
12	carbon
13	slate, concrete
14	glass, porcelain,
15½	quartzite, flint
20	all animals, plants wood, rubber, coal, paper, bread, potatoes
22	silver, lead, salt
23½	vegetable oil, amber
24	masculinity, diamond
25½	alcohol
26½	running water
29	femininity, gold
30½	copper, brass, tin
32	iron
40	Death

?

Above: table of pendulum 'rates' as discovered by Tom Lethbridge in the course of his experiments. Through trial and error he came to realise that the pendulum reacted consistently at certain lengths to specific substances, qualities and even abstract ideas

Left and right: mended pots that had been found in fragments in the courtyard and orchard of Hole House solely through dowsing. Lethbridge dowsed them to find their ages, finally coming up with the dates he scratched on the bottoms. Lethbridge achieved a high degree of accuracy – his dates for certain standing stones, for example, were later proved to be correct by carbon dating. As he said 'It may seem absurd, but it delivers the goods'

reasoned that because 'our world' – that is, the world that registers below 40 – is in time, there is no reaction to the idea of time itself – just as you could not appreciate the speed of a river if you were drifting down at the same speed as the current. But there is a reaction to the idea of time in this 'world beyond death'. Moreover, Lethbridge found that if he lengthened the pendulum beyond 80, he got the same result all over again – as if there is yet another world – or dimension – beyond that one. And this 'third world' also has a reaction for time. But when Lethbridge lengthened the pendulum beyond 120 inches he discovered that the 'world' beyond that also had no reaction for time.

Secrets of the 'other you'

Tom Lethbridge's own explanation of this strange 'power of the pendulum' is that there is a part of the human mind – the unconscious, perhaps – that knows the answers to all questions. Unfortunately, it cannot convey these answers to the 'everyday you', the busy, conscious self that spends its time coping with practical problems. But this 'other you' *can* convey its messages via the dowsing rod or pendulum, by the simple expedient of controlling the muscles.

Lethbridge had started as a cheerfully sceptical investigator trying to understand nature's hidden codes for conveying information. His researches led him into strange,

bewildering realms where all his normal ideas seemed to be turned upside down. He compared himself to a man walking on ice, when it suddenly collapses and he finds himself floundering in freezing water. Of this sudden immersion in new ideas he said: 'From living a normal life in a three-dimensional world, I seem to have suddenly fallen through into one where there are more dimensions. The three-dimensional life goes on as usual; but one has to adjust one's thinking to the other.' He did more than adjust his thinking; he set out boldly to explore the fourth dimension – and came to highly significant conclusions.

Gateway to other worlds

Tom Lethbridge progressed from finding hidden objects through dowsing to exploring the timeless world beyond death.

IN 1962, FIVE YEARS AFTER his move to Devon, Tom Lethbridge's ideas on ghosts, 'ghouls', pendulums and dowsing rods began to crystallise into a coherent theory, which he outlined in a book called *Ghost and divining rod*. This appeared in 1963, and it aroused more interest than anything he had published so far. It deserved to be so popular, for its central theory was original, exciting and well-argued.

He suggested that nature generates fields of static electricity in certain places, particularly near running water. These 'fields' are capable of picking up and recording the thoughts and feelings of human beings and other living creatures. But human beings are also surrounded by a mild electrical field, as the researches of Harold Burr of Yale University in the United States revealed in the 1930s. So if someone goes into a room where a murder has taken place and experiences a distinctly unpleasant feeling, all that is happening is that the emotions associated with the crime (such as fear, pain and horror) are being transferred to the visitor's electrical field, in accordance with the laws of electricity. If we are feeling full of energy, excitement, misery or anger, the emotional transference may flow the other way, and our feelings will be recorded on the field.

But if human emotions can be imprinted in some way on the 'field' of running water, and picked up by a dowser, then this world we are living in is a far more strange and

Above: Tom Lethbridge cataloguing some archaeological finds

Below: Saddell Abbey, Strathclyde, Scotland – a place of curiously strong and varied atmospheres: menacing in the castle, melancholy in the abbey ruins and peaceful at the wishing well. Lethbridge believed that 'atmospheres' are powerful emotions 'recorded' in the electrical field of water

complex place than most people give it credit for. To begin with, we must be surrounded by hidden information – in the form of these 'tape recordings' – that might become accessible to all of us if we could master the art of using the dowser's pendulum.

It looks – says Lethbridge – as if human beings possess 'psyche-fields' as well as bodies. The body is simply a piece of apparatus for collecting impressions, which are then stored in the psyche-field. But in that case, there would seem to be a part of us that seeks the information. Presumably this is what religious people call the spirit. And since the information it can acquire through the pendulum may come from the remote past, or from some place on the other side of the world, then this spirit must be outside the limits of space and time.

It was this last idea that excited Lethbridge so much. His experiments with the pendulum seemed to indicate that there are other worlds beyond this one, perhaps worlds in other dimensions. Presumably we cannot see them – although they co-exist with our world – because our bodies are rather crude machines for picking up low-level vibrations. But the psyche-field – or perhaps the spirit – seems to have access to these other invisible worlds.

It also seems to have access to other times and other places. In May 1964, a BBC camera

team went to Hole House to record an interview with Lethbridge about dowsing. A young cameraman looked so dazed and start-led as he got out of the car that Lethbridge asked him: 'Have you been here before?' The cameraman shook his head. 'No. But I've dreamed about it.' He asked if he could look behind the house. Pointing to a wall that Lethbridge had knocked down and rebuilt, he said: 'It wasn't like that years ago. There used to be buildings against it.' That was true – but not in Lethbridge's time. In the herb garden, the cameraman said: 'There used to be buildings there, but they were pulled down.' In his dream a voice had said, 'Now we shall be able to see the sea.' Again, it was true – but many years before, at the turn of the century. Now a row of trees blotted out the view of the sea.

The cameraman had never been in the area before, and he had no friends or relatives there who might have told him about it. Yet on five occasions he had dreamed about Hole House – as it was before he was born.

Lethbridge had always been interested in dreams, ever since he read J.W. Dunne's *An experiment with time* in the 1930s. Dunne was an aeronautics engineer, and around the turn of the century he had a number of impressive dreams of the future – for example, he dreamed accurately about the forthcoming eruption of the volcano, Mount Pelée, on Martinique. Dunne had suggested that time is like a tape or a film, which may get twisted or tangled, so that we can catch glimpses of

Above: diagram illustrating Lethbridge's theory about the creation of the world-wide belief in nymphs:
1. Aroused youth, pausing within the static field of a stream (A), vividly creates the image of a girl bathing (C) in his own static field (B). The image leaks into the weaker field (A) where it is 'recorded'.
2. Perhaps years later a passing youth with a weak psyche-field (D) comes into contact with (A) from which the image of the girl (C) leaks into his field (D). He thinks he has witnessed a supernatural being when he has really only seen the recording of a thoughtform

Right: eruption of the volcanic Mount Pelée, Martinique. J. W. Dunne, author of *An experiment with time*, had dreamed accurately of the event some time before it happened. This and other dreams convinced him that we dream regularly of future events but do not always remember these dreams

other times. He used to keep a notebook and pencil by his bed, and jot down his dreams the moment he woke up. He was convinced that we all dream about the future – probably every night of our lives – but that we forget it almost as soon as we wake up.

Lethbridge decided that if he wanted to study this mystery of dreams, he should keep a dream notebook. It was soon filled with his own vivid and idiosyncratic observations.

He became convinced that Dunne was correct in believing that we all dream of future events, but that most of these are so trivial – or so brief – that we fail to remember them. One night, he woke up dreaming about the face of a man that seemed to be looking at him out of a mirror. He was doing something with his hands, which seemed to be moving in the area of his chin. Lethbridge thought he might be shaving.

The next day, Lethbridge was driving slowly along a narrow lane; a car came round the corner, and at the wheel was the man he had seen in his dream. His face was framed by the windscreen – which Lethbridge had mistaken for a mirror – and his hands were moving in the area of his chin, on top of the steering wheel. Lethbridge was certain that he had never seen the man before.

He also noted that some of his dreams seemed to go backwards. He once dreamed of a furry snake-like object coming into his bed-room; but all the furniture in the room was reversed, as in a mirror. The snake-like object he recognised as the tail of their Siamese cat, walking backwards. A friend also told him about two 'backward dreams' she had had recently: in one, she saw a couple she knew walk backwards out of their door and drive their car backwards down a lane. In another, she saw some men walking back-wards carrying a coffin, and one of them uttered the baffling sentence: 'Burnt be to

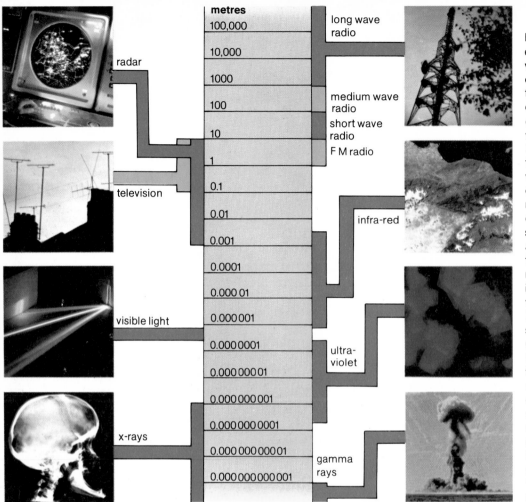

radar

television

visible light

x-rays

metres	
100,000	long wave radio
10,000	
1000	
100	medium wave radio
10	short wave radio
1	FM radio
0.1	
0.01	
0.001	infra-red
0.0001	
0.000 01	
0.000001	
0.0000001	ultra-violet
0.000 000 01	
0.000 000 001	
0.000 000 0001	
0.000 000 000 01	gamma rays
0.000 000 000 001	

Left: the spectrum of electromagnetic (EM) vibrations. EM waves consist of electric and magnetic fields vibrating with a definite frequency, each corresponding to a particular wavelength.
In order of increasing frequency and decreasing wavelength, the EM spectrum consists of: very long wave radio, used for communication with submarines; long, medium and short wave radio (used for AM broadcasting); FM radio, television and radar; infra-red (heat) radiation, which is recorded in the Earth photographs taken by survey satellites; visible light; ultraviolet light, which, while invisible, stimulates fluorescence in some materials; x-rays; and high-energy gamma rays, which occur in fallout and in cosmic rays. The progressive discovery of these waves has inspired speculations concerning unknown 'vibrations' making up our own and higher worlds

enough good woods any.' On waking up, she wrote down the sentence, read it backwards, and realised that it actually said: 'Any wood's good enough to be burnt.'

But why, Lethbridge asked, should time sometimes go backwards in dreams? The clue was provided by his pendulum, which informed him that the energy vibrations of the next level – the world beyond ours – are four times as fast as those of our world. Lethbridge speculated that during sleep, a part of us passes through this world to a higher world still. Coming back from sleep, we pass through it once again to enter our own much slower world of vibrations. The effect is like a fast train passing a slower one; although the slow train is moving forward, it appears to be going backwards.

More impressive examples of precognitive dreams came from his correspondents. One woman dreamed of the collapse of a building as the side was blown out and heard a voice say: 'Collapsed like a pack of cards.' A month later a gas explosion blew out the side of a block of flats called Ronan Point in East London, and a newspaper report used the phrase 'Collapsed like a pack of cards'. Another correspondent described a dream in which he saw a square-looking Edwardian house with many chimneys being burnt down; a few days later, Tom saw a house of

The ruined London tower block, Ronan Point. A gas explosion ripped through the building causing death and devastation. One woman dreamed precognitively of the disaster, hearing the very words of the subsequent newspaper headline 'Collapsed like a pack of cards' spoken clearly

this description being burnt down on a television newsreel.

The more he studied these puzzles, the more convinced Lethbridge became that the key to all of them is the concept of *vibrations*. Our bodies seem to be machines tuned to pick up certain vibrations. Our eyes will only register energy whose wavelength is between that of red and violet light. Shorter or longer wavelengths are invisible to us. Modern physics tells us that at the sub-atomic level matter is in a state of constant vibration.

Worlds beyond worlds

According to Lethbridge's pendulum, the 'world' beyond our world – the world that can be detected by a pendulum of more than 40 inches – consists of vibrations that are four times as fast as ours. It is all around us yet we are unable to see it, because it is beyond the range of our senses. All the objects in our world extend into this other world. Our personalities also extend into it, but we are not aware of this, because our 'everyday self' has no communication with that 'other self'. But the other self can answer questions by means of the pendulum. When Tom and Mina Lethbridge visited a circle of standing stones called the Merry Maidens, near Penzance in Cornwall, Lethbridge held a pendulum over one of the uprights and asked how old it was. As he did so, he placed one hand on the stone, and experienced something like a mild electric shock. The pendulum began to gyrate like an aeroplane propellor, and went on swinging in a wide circle for several minutes – Lethbridge counted 451 turns. Arbitrarily allowing 10 years for each turn, Lethbridge calculated that the circle dated back to 2540 BC – a result that sounds highly consistent with carbon 14 dating of other megalithic monuments like Stonehenge. His 'higher self' – outside time – had answered his question.

In 1971 Lethbridge was engaged in writing his book on dreams – *The power of the pendulum* – when he became ill and had to be taken into hospital. He was a huge man, and his enormous weight placed a strain on his heart. He died on 30 September, leaving his last book unrevised. He was 70 years old, and his life's work was by no means complete. Yet even in its unfinished state, it is one of the

The ancient circle of standing stones known as the Merry Maidens near Penzance, Cornwall. While dowsing over the stones Lethbridge experienced a mild electric shock as if the stones were some kind of battery. But, persisting with his pendulum, he was able to dowse for the age of the stones. Later, more sophisticated techniques – such as carbon 14 dating – were used to date the Merry Maidens and Lethbridge's dating was confirmed

most important and exciting contributions to parapsychology in this century.

Lethbridge's insistence on rediscovering the ancient art of dowsing also underlined his emphasis on understanding the differences between primitive and modern Man. The ancient peoples – going back to our cavemen ancestors – believed that the Universe is magical and that Earth is a living creature. They were probably natural dowsers – as the aborigines of Australia still are – and responded naturally to the forces of the earth. Their standing stones were, according to Lethbridge, intended to mark places where the earth force was most powerful and perhaps to harness it in some way now forgotten.

Modern Man has suppressed – or lost – that instinctive, intuitive contact with the forces of the Universe. He is too busy keeping together his precious civilisation. Yet he still potentially possesses that ancient power of dowsing, and could easily develop it if he really wanted to. Lethbridge set out to develop his own powers, and to explore them scientifically, and soon came to the conclusion that the dowsing rod and the pendulum are incredibly accurate. By making use of some unknown part of the mind – the unconscious or 'superconscious' – they can provide information that is inaccessible to our ordinary senses, and can tell us about realms of reality beyond the 'everyday' world of physical matter.

Lethbridge was not a spiritualist. He never paid much attention to the question of life after death or the existence of a 'spirit world'. But by pursuing his researches into these subjects with a tough-minded logic, he concluded that there are other realms of reality beyond our world, and that there are forms of energy that we do not even begin to understand. Magic, spiritualism and occultism are merely our crude attempts to understand this vast realm of hidden energies, just as alchemy was Man's earliest attempt to understand the mysteries of atomic physics.

As to the meaning of all this, Lethbridge preserves the caution of an academic. Yet in his last years he became increasingly convinced that there is a meaning in human existence, and that it is tied up with the concept of our personal evolution. For some reason, we are being *driven* to evolve.

Eileen Garrett

A thoroughly modern medium

Few Spiritualist mediums have questioned the otherworldly origin of their powers, but Eileen Garrett, one of the most gifted, had her doubts. ROY STEMMAN tells the story of this unusually objective psychic

EILEEN GARRETT has been described as 'probably the most thoroughly investigated medium of modern times'. The reason, quite apart from her exceptional psychic talents, was that she devoted most of her life to encouraging research into mediumship and its meaning, frequently offering herself as the first psychic guinea-pig in experiments.

Her powers ranged from clairvoyance and astral projection to physical mediumship. But it was as a trance medium – apparently allowing the dead to speak through her lips – that she made the greatest impact. It was in this manner that she was used as a channel for

Eileen Garrett as a young woman. Brought up against a background of sectarian strife in Ireland she soon rejected religion, and even after she became a famous medium she was frequently irritated by the dogmatic assertions of many Spiritualists. She was eager to be scientifically investigated in the hope that more could be discovered about the human psyche

communications allegedly from the captain of the British airship *R101*, Flight-Lieutenant H.C. Irwin, in 1930: a remarkable case that many still regard as among the best in providing evidence for life after death.

But Mrs Garrett was more reticent about her mediumship than others. She accepted that the content of her trance communications was paranormal in origin, but she was open-minded about 'the dead' who spoke through her. This ambiguous approach to her mediumship extended to the spirit 'controls' who worked through her, each of whom had a distinct personality. There was Uvani, who claimed to have been a soldier in India centuries ago, and Abdul Latif, a 12th-century physician from the court of Saladin, whose particular interest was healing. In the early days of her mediumship Mrs Garrett accepted them as spirit helpers, but in time she began to doubt this and believed, instead, that they might be secondary personalities produced by her own subconscious.

Split personalities?

In an attempt to find the truth Mrs Garrett willingly participated in experiments designed to compare these trance personalities with her own waking personality. The investigators spent many hours talking to Uvani and Abdul Latif – even using word association tests on the spirit controls and the medium. However, these tests were inconclusive. One investigator decided that Uvani was probably a 'split-off' personality from the medium – indeed, Uvani himself said he manipulated a split-off portion of Mrs Garrett's unconscious. Another researcher concluded that the two spirit controls were independent personalities.

Mrs Garrett's own opinion in later life, given in her autobiography *Many voices* (1968), was:

> I prefer to think of the controls as principals of the subconscious. I had, unconsciously, adopted them by name and during the years of early training. I respect them, but cannot explain them.
> . . . The controls are well aware that I have maintained an impartial, but respectful, attitude towards my own work and theirs, and so the search continues.

Later, she added, 'I have never been able wholly to accept them as the spiritual dwellers on the threshold, which they seem to believe they are.'

The mystery deepened with the surfacing of two more controls. One, named Tehotah, claimed to be an entity that personified the Logos or divine word, while Rama was said to be the personification of the life force.

in experiments into ESP.

New York psychologist Lawrence LeShan spent more than 500 hours questioning Mrs Garrett about her psychic abilities, then designed several experiments to test them thoroughly. One was a psychometry test in which the medium was asked to hold various objects and give her clairvoyant impressions about them.

The objects included a fossil fish, a scrap of bandage, a piece of stone from Mount Vesuvius, an old Greek coin and an ancient Babylonian clay tablet. Each was wrapped in tissue, then placed in a box that, in turn, was put inside a manila envelope and numbered. Another person then put these numbered envelopes inside larger envelopes, marking them with a different number. As a result, no one knew which object was inside which envelope.

During preparations for this experiment a secretary picked up the Babylonian tablet and examined it. Two weeks later, when LeShan conducted the experiment with Mrs Garrett 1500 miles (2400 kilometres) away in

Left: New York psychologist Lawrence LeShan was impressed with Mrs Garrett's psychic gifts and her analytical intelligence. He investigated her thoroughly; during one psychometry experiment LeShan was amazed when Mrs Garrett, picking up an envelope containing the target object – an ancient Babylonian tablet (below) – not only described it accurately but proceeded to give a detailed description of the secretary who had originally parcelled it up

Neither had incarnated as an individual.

Eileen Garrett was born in County Meath, in the Republic of Ireland, on 17 March 1893, the daughter of Anne Brownell and a Spaniard named Vancho. Two weeks later her mother drowned herself and a few weeks after that her father also committed suicide: the double tragedy created, apparently, by the pressures of Protestant and Catholic conflicts. As a result, Eileen was brought up by an uncle and aunt – who were Protestant, but no bigots.

A late uncle's advice

Like so many other sensitive children – and in particular natural psychics – Eileen had playmates who were invisible to others. But the most impressive paranormal experience of those early years concerned her uncle, who had been extremely kind and understanding to her. A couple of weeks after his death Eileen saw him standing before her 'looking young, erect and strong'. He said that he understood the difficulties of her present life. Then he predicted that she would go to London to study in two years – which is exactly what happened. He then vanished before she could ask any questions. It was from that moment that Eileen became interested in the question of survival of death.

In time she encountered Spiritualism and began developing her psychic gifts – particularly trance mediumship – under the guidance of James Hewat McKenzie at the British College of Psychic Science. As a result, she provided many bereaved people with impressive evidence for survival.

In 1931 the American Society for Psychical Research invited her to New York to give sittings, and she also worked with Professor William McDougall and Dr J.B. Rhine at Duke University, North Carolina,

Right: Professor William McDougall who, together with Dr J.B. Rhine, conducted experiments with Eileen Garrett at Duke University in North Carolina, USA

Left: Cecil B. de Mille, director of epic films and a notoriously tough character; nevertheless he was reduced to tears when Mrs Garrett described an old lady she 'saw' standing next to him. It was a perfect description of his dead mother

Florida, she picked up an envelope and said immediately that there was 'a woman associated with this'.

It was later found that this envelope contained the clay tablet, and Mrs Garrett's description of the woman so perfectly matched the secretary who had handled it that, according to LeShan, it would have been possible 'to pick her out of a line-up of 10,000 women'. The medium even mentioned two scars that the woman had.

During the experiments with her, LeShan learned indirectly of a man who had vanished from a mid western city in the USA. He gave Mrs Garrett, in New York, a square of cloth cut from one of the man's shirts and asked for her impressions. The medium gave a fairly accurate description of the missing man, whose appearance was, at that time, unknown to LeShan, adding that he had had a loss in his family between the ages of 13 and

Below: Eileen Garrett was a prolific writer and a dynamic personality. Here she surveys some of the books written by or about her

Below right: after Mrs Garrett's death in 1970 her daughter continued her work through the Parapsychological Foundation, which Eileen founded in 1951

15. It was discovered that his father had deserted the family when he was 14 and had not been heard of since. She also said that the man was in La Jolla, California, and it was confirmed later that he had gone there after leaving his home.

A spontaneous phenomenon of a physical kind occurred in 1931 when Mrs Garrett was lying on an operating table in hospital. Just after she succumbed to the anaesthetic, the doctors and nurses in attendance heard a voice. Her physician, who had been in India in his youth, told her later that he recognised certain definite words of command, as spoken in Hindustani. Because of the way Mrs Garrett had been prepared for the operation the doctor knew that it was quite impossible for her to utter a sound. He was so impressed by the experience that he sent a letter to various Spiritualist leaders putting the circumstances on record.

Eileen Garrett was far removed from the popular, otherworldly, image of a medium. She had a vivacious personality and a questing spirit, and in addition to her psychic work she also ran a tea room, a workers' hostel and eventually a literary magazine, *Tomorrow*, which she later changed to deal entirely with psychic matters.

She married three times, lost three sons – one at birth and two through illness. Her daughter continues her work through the Parapsychology Foundation, which Eileen Garrett founded in New York in 1951.

Eileen Garrett died at Le Piol, France, in 1970, having made an enormous personal contribution to psychical research. She had no doubt about the reality of paranormal phenomena. What she *did* doubt was the spirit hypothesis of mediumship that so many accept blindly. And by setting up the Parapsychology Foundation she ensured that the search for some understanding of the nature of psychic phenomena would continue long after her death.

Doris Stokes is, she says, a perfectly ordinary, down-to-earth person. But she has a special gift, which enables her to hear the dead speak. ROY STEMMAN looks at the life and work of the woman whose exceptional psychic powers have brought comfort to thousands of people

DORIS STOKES'S appearance on Australian television caused a sensation. The switchboard was flooded with calls, letters poured in, and Channel 9 took off *Starsky & Hutch* to make room for a second hour-long programme about this daughter of an English blacksmith.

No other personality had had such an impact on Australian viewers, yet Doris Stokes is not a superstar. She lives with her husband John in a modest London flat and regards herself as a very ordinary person. But she has an unusual gift that sets her apart from others: she is a medium who claims to be able to speak with the dead.

After being interviewed by Don Lane on his popular television variety show, Doris Stokes was invited to give messages to members of his studio audience. It is something

Doris Stokes appears on Australian television in the *Don Lane Show* (right). As a result of the programme Doris received thousands of telephone calls and hundreds of letters, and went on a whirlwind tour of Australia. She was staggered at this response from the public and told the crowds: 'I'm nothing special. Please don't get the wrong impression. I'm just the same as you are'

The medium and the message

she does regularly in Spiritualist churches in England without creating much of a stir – but for most Australian television viewers the spectacle of a woman 'speaking' to spirits was astonishing. They demanded more and Australian television was happy to oblige. 'A [psychic] star was born', her visit to Australia was extended, and soon a tour of major cities was organised during which the largest halls – including the Sydney Opera House – were packed with people eager to see her in action and perhaps receive a personal message.

What is it about Doris Stokes that created such a reaction? It is the direct and confident way in which she acts as a 'go-between', relaying names and information that she says are given to her by the dead. Much of this she hears as voices – different in accent and intonation – and so she is known as a *clairaudient*, rather than a *clairvoyant* (a medium whose impressions are visual).

In the television studio her down-to-earth, good-humoured manner ensured that there was nothing 'spooky' about her performance. She simply stood in front of her audience and waited for the voices to give her information.

'The lady over there,' she said, pointing to one of Don Lane's studio guests. 'I've got a man here called Bert.'

'That's my brother-in-law,' the woman gasped.

'He says he went over very quickly.'

'That's right.'

'Who's Wyn?'

'I'm Wyn.'

The messages she gives are usually made

up of such trivia, but the accuracy of the names and details leave her recipients in no doubt that they are witnessing a paranormal phenomenon. Guesswork alone would not explain the content of the messages. But is it really communication with the dead or is she just using extra-sensory perception (ESP)? That is something that each person has to decide for himself, just as Doris Stokes had to decide in her early days.

Her psychic gifts were apparent from an early age when she found herself describing – or predicting – things that she could not have known normally. This worried her mother, but her father – a natural psychic like his daughter – understood and did nothing to discourage her. It was not until after Doris was married and her father had died that her psychic powers grew stronger: and her experiences left her in no doubt that she was in contact with people who had died.

A visit from the dead

Her most dramatic personal experience occurred during the Second World War. Her husband was reported 'missing in action' and a medium at a local Spiritualist church in Grantham, Lincolnshire, 'confirmed' that he had been killed. Doris Stokes returned home to her baby son in a state of shock. She describes what happened next in her autobiography, *Voices in my ear*:

> Then the bedroom door flew open so sharply I thought it was mother bursting in and there stood my father. My mouth dropped open. He looked as real and as solid as he did when he was alive . . .
> 'Dad?' I whispered.
> 'I never lied to you, did I, Doll?' he asked.
> 'I don't think so,' I said.
> 'I'm not lying to you now. John is not with us and on Christmas Day you will have proof of this.' Then as I watched, he vanished.

Three days later came a letter from the War Office telling her that John was dead. But while everyone else mourned, the 'widow' refused to believe it. Her dead father was proved right, however. Just as he had predicted she learned that John was still alive, though wounded and a prisoner of war, on Christmas Day.

Doris was never trained as a medium, although she once attended a Spiritualist 'development circle' – and was appallingly embarrassed. First, she was shown into a room of 'cranky old dears clucking admiringly about a bossy medium.' They all then sat quietly, with their eyes shut, waiting for the spirit world to communicate with them. But Doris's eyes flew open again when a large lady stood up and majestically announced, in a deep voice, but still unmistakably her own, that she was 'Chief Sitting Bull'. Doris could hardly believe it – all these people taking this patent nonsense so seriously! And then

'Chief Sitting Bull' addressed some very stern words to her; she had to uncross her legs and keep her feet on the ground 'to earth the power'. Doris remarked that she was made to feel like a human light bulb and found it all quite ridiculous. She never went back.

However, she had no need for training. It soon became apparent that her special, psychic gifts could give comfort and practical help to the bereaved and the despairing. She began to give 'seances' – although that rather spooky and old-fashioned word sounds very odd in conjunction with Doris – both on public platforms and in private houses. She never promises to 'get through' to any particular person on the 'other side', but settles the audience down, confident that the spirits will eventually speak to them through her. They have very rarely let her down.

She has found that the longer a person has

Top: Tom Sutton, Doris's father. He died when Doris was a young girl, but 'visited' her twice several years later during the Second World War. On the first occasion he told her that her husband John (above) – reported missing in action – was alive and would return. The second time he warned her that her healthy infant son was soon to die. Both 'predictions' were accurate

been dead, the stronger his or her voice seems to be – those newly 'passed over' tend to sound faint. Sometimes the voices fade away altogether. She has now learned to cope with these silent phases but in her early days she was tempted to cheat. Doris Stokes must be one of the few practising mediums to admit to it.

She was young and felt very 'special' because of her strange abilities and was therefore inclined to show off. When the voices stopped, leaving her alone and unaided on a platform in front of a packed house, she was eager to heed the advice of an experienced 'circuit' medium. Get to the meetings early, he suggested, and listen in to the conversations of the audience. You're bound to pick up a few hints, names, dates and so on. People will always talk about their hopes – in this case the spirits they hope to 'hear' from through Doris. Take down some notes surreptitiously, he said, then if your voices stop abruptly you can consult them and 'fudge' the messages. That way your audience will leave happy.

Doris admits that she tried cheating in this way, twice. The first time she slipped her notes into her hymn book, hoping she would not have to use them. But gradually – in the middle of a message for a lady in the audience – the voices stopped. White-faced, Doris fumbled for her notes – but they had disappeared. Somehow, remembering bits of what she had overheard and making up the rest, she finished the 'communication' but noticed that the lady seemed a little bewildered – it was such a muddle. But the worst was yet to come.

Just as abruptly as they had departed, the voices came back. Doris managed two real messages then was aware that her spirit guide – whose name approximates to the English spelling Ramononov – had taken over and was saying 'Now we'll go back to Mrs . . .' (the lady whose message had just been faked) 'and you'll apologise to her and tell her that the last part of the message didn't came from the spirit world'.

Horrified at being faced with a public humiliation, Doris hesitated, then plunged in: 'I'm terribly sorry. I've got to tell you the last bit of your message didn't come from the spirit. That was me.'

Advice from the other side

People who seek help from mediums are mostly the grief-stricken bereaved. What raises Doris Stokes above the run-of-the-mill Spiritualist medium is her extraordinary down-to-earth attitude. To her the spirit world is as real as this one – and her firm conviction of survival after death communicates itself to her audience. Her specific and often deeply personalised messages purporting to come from the dead frequently offer urgent advice: one deeply depressed widower was told by his wife not to take the overdose he was planning. He was impressed by the fact that no one knew of his intentions except himself – that, and the anger Doris conveyed from his wife. 'Your wife is very anxious about you. She says that is not the way. You must not do it. She's waiting for you and if she's gone on she'll make sure of being there to meet you when your time comes, but you must wait until your time comes, or you will regret it.'

Many a medium could have trotted out that advice – for almost all religious people are opposed to suicide – but Doris backed this up by 'proving' the continued existence of the man's wife through conveying many personal pieces of information that only the widower and his wife could have known.

There are occasions, however, when Doris herself needs the help of psychics. One such time was when she was 33, and, her first

Below: Walter Brookes, the medium who gave Doris a message warning her of a forthcoming illness

Above: Doris 'performs' before the studio audience of Tyne Tees Television's *Friday Live* programme in December 1979

child having died, she was hoping to become pregnant again. One day she was talking to a friend, Walter Brookes, a well-known Yorkshire medium, when he suddenly asked if she had just come out of hospital. No, said Doris, who was feeling fit and well.

'Just a minute,' he said. 'This is serious. I'm afraid you're going into hospital – July I think, something to do with your right side. They'll say you're going to die, but your father wants you to write this down. It's the name of the person you must ask for. Mrs Marrow.'

That July Doris Stokes was suddenly stricken with agonising pain in her stomach. She was rushed to hospital where it was found that pregnancy had occurred in one of her Fallopian tubes. John Stokes was told there was nothing that could be done for her. She was dying.

Remembering the message from Doris's dead father, John Stokes asked the doctors if they knew a Mrs Marrow. When he learned they did and that she was a gynaecologist at a Nottingham hospital he insisted that his wife be transferred. There, under Mrs Marrow's expert care, Doris recovered. And soon she was able to resume her work as a medium, relaying messages that may well have saved the lives of others.

Following the success of her first visit to Australia, Doris returned in 1980 for an equally triumphant tour, with television and radio appearances.

Spiritualism's critics, of course, are not pleased that mediums such as Doris Stokes are allowed to demonstrate their powers to such a wide audience. But Doris is happy to be judged by the results of her work – and they speak for themselves.

Ted Serios in focus

Can thoughts really be photographed? Chicago bell-hop Ted Serios believes they can, and has produced hundreds of pictures as proof. ROY STEMMAN considers the claims made by, and for, this psychic photographer – and examines the sceptics' attempts to expose him

TED SERIOS SAT DOWN in the hotel room and pointed a Polaroid camera at his face. The flashbulb fired and Dr Jule Eisenbud immediately took the camera from him and pulled the print from the back. Instead of showing Serios's face the unmistakable image of a building appeared.

For Serios, a chain-smoking, alcoholic Chicago bell-hop, it was just another of his strange psychic photographs that he calls 'thoughtographs'. But for Dr Eisenbud, an associate professor of psychiatry at the University of Colorado Medical School, it was such an impressive demonstration of paranormal power that he went on to study Serios for several years and write a book about him.

When he flew to Chicago for the first experimental session with the hard-drinking psychic photographer in April 1964, Eisenbud was almost certain that he was about to witness 'some kind of shoddy hoax'. Because of his interest in the paranormal, Eisenbud was aware that there had been many so-called psychic photographers over the years who had been caught cheating, usually by tampering with the film. The appearance of the Polaroid camera had changed that, making it easier to control the production of such 'thoughtographic' prints as well as giving results in seconds.

Investigators who have worked with Serios supply their own film and cameras;

Right: one of the few colour 'thoughtographs' produced by Serios. He was aiming at a target picture of the Hilton hotel at Denver, but obtained this image of the Chicago Hilton instead

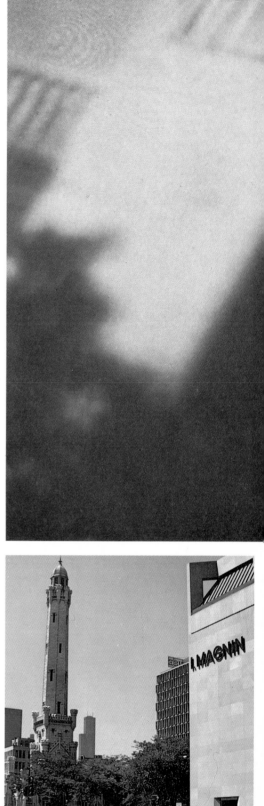

Below: the first picture of a 'recognisable structure' that Serios produced for researcher Dr Jule Eisenbud. It was immediately identified by one of the observers at the session as the Chicago Water Tower (below right)

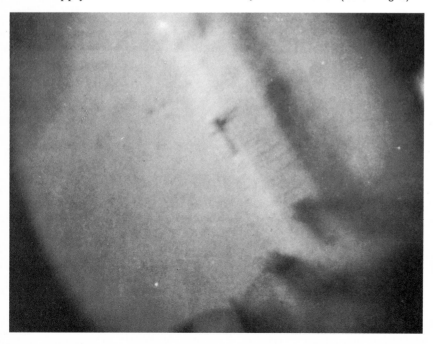

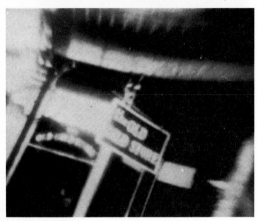

Above: one of eleven views of a shop front in Central City, Colorado, produced by Serios (left) in 1965. At that time the building was used as a tourist shop called the 'Old Wells Fargo Express Office', but several years before it was 'The Old Gold Store', no photographs of which were known to exist. In one of the pictures (top), the billing reads 'The Wld Gold Store': to create this effect fraudulently, Serios would have had to use two transparencies

sometimes they even take the pictures themselves, with the camera pointing at the Chicago psychic – and yet, the results that emerge are frequently very strange indeed. Not all the photographs carry images; some are unusually white while others are totally and inexplicably black, even though the room lighting and other factors remain constant. Occasionally, the image that emerges from the Polaroid covers the whole area of the print while at other times it obliterates only a portion of Serios or identifiable items in the room where the experiment is being conducted.

Can Serios really impress his thoughts on photographs? It is so unlikely that the possibility of a cunning fraud has to be looked at from the start, and sceptics do not need to look very far to have their suspicions aroused. In his early days, Serios just looked at the camera to produce his startling pictures, but later he introduced a 'gismo', which he holds in front of the lens while concentrating. Sometimes he uses a small plastic cylinder, one end of which is covered with plain cellophane, the other with cellophane over a piece of blackened film; on other occasions he simply rolls up a piece of paper.

The purpose of the 'gismo', says Serios, is to keep his fingers from obscuring the lens. His critics, however, see it as having a far more sinister purpose. It could very easily conceal a 'gimmick' containing microfilm or transparency, they argue, and for them it is as suspicious as a conjuror's hat.

Two reporters, Charles Reynolds and David Eisendrath, constructed a small device that could be hidden in a 'gismo' and that produced similar-looking results to those of Serios. Their account, published in *Popular Photography* in October 1967, gave the sceptics the 'evidence' they needed.

Secrets of the 'gismo'

Eisenbud and other researchers, on the other hand, are satisfied that the 'gismo' contains no hidden equipment, nor does Serios slip anything inside it just before an exposure is made. They are all aware of the hidden microfilm hypothesis and have evolved an experimental protocol to overcome it. Serios is usually given the 'gismo' when he feels he can produce a paranormal print. It is then taken from him immediately and examined. It is probably in his hands for no longer than 15 seconds at a time and throughout that period it is under close scrutiny.

Serios usually wears short-sleeved shirts or strips to the waist, making it impossible for him to conceal anything close to his hands. Besides, say the researchers, they are frequently close enough to the action when Serios tells them to fire the camera that they can actually see through the 'gismo' and *know* that it contains no hidden devices.

On numerous occasions images appeared when someone else was holding the 'gismo' and the camera, and able to examine both freely. Two eminent American psychical researchers, Dr J. G. Pratt and Dr Ian Stevenson, who conducted numerous tests with Serios, have stated: 'We have ourselves observed Ted in approximately 800 trials and we have never seen him act in a suspicious way in the handling of the gismo before or after a trial.' Quite apart from the fact that Serios has never been caught with any hidden transparencies or microfilm, Dr Eisenbud argues that the very nature of the images that Serios produces rules out the 'gimmick' theory.

Serios invited investigators to bring with them target pictures concealed in envelopes, which he tried to reproduce on Polaroid film paranormally. On the first occasion that

change, says Eisenbud, must have occurred no later than 1958 and possibly earlier, and research has failed to unearth any photographs of the store in its earlier days.

But, although Serios's paranormal picture corresponds perfectly (but for the name) with the present-day store, there is a curious substitution in one picture of the letter 'W' for 'O' so that it reads 'The Wld Gold Store'. And the 'W' is exactly where it would be if 'Wells Fargo' had been spelled out.

Something similar happened with a picture that showed two storeys of a building and some slightly out-of-focus lettering that was, nevertheless, discernible. The building was ultimately acknowledged by the Royal Canadian Mounted Police as one of their Air Division hangars, but they pointed out a curious misspelling, which other observers had also noted. The words in Serios's picture read 'Air Division *Cainadain* Moun——'.

If Serios were somehow using concealed transparencies to produce his pictures then he was also having to tamper with the

Eisenbud saw Serios produce a paranormal picture, in a Chicago hotel room, the psychiatrist had taken with him two views of the Kremlin buildings, each hidden in a cardboard-backed manila envelope.

One of the images that Serios produced at this session was of a tall, thin building, which one of the witnesses immediately identified as the Chicago Water Tower – a landmark that would have been familiar to Serios. Though this seemed to be totally off target, Eisenbud was very impressed, partly because some of the images and symbols in the picture were relevant to a line of thought that was in his mind at the time.

Two years later, however, Eisenbud came across another view of the Kremlin buildings and this time Ivan's Bell Tower, which was only partly visible in one of the two target pictures, was prominent. It was only then that he realised that it has 'an easily discernible resemblance' to the Chicago Water Tower. Serios, it seems, scored a hit after all.

But stranger things have happened. In May 1965 Serios produced 11 slightly different versions of what appeared to be a plate glass store front. On two of them the name 'The Old Gold Store' is clearly visible in bold block lettering. Two years later the place was recognised as a tourist shop in Central City, Colorado, which is now the 'Old Wells Fargo Express Office'. The name

Top: the blurred lettering on this 'thoughtograph' enabled researchers to identify the building as a hangar belonging to the Air Division of the Royal Canadian Mounted Police (above). The picture bears the unmistakable stamp of Ted Serios in the misspelling 'CAINADAIN'

originals in an expert way to come up with such bizarre images. Another very clear picture showed Williams's Livery Stable, across the street from the Opera House in Central City. But there were strange distortions. The brickwork had changed: in Serios's picture it was like imbedded rock whereas the building is in fact constructed of pressed brick. Also, the windows in the paranormal print were bricked up.

Because of such pictures, in which Serios seems to be photographing the past (and distorting reality, too), Eisenbud and some fellow researchers arranged an experimental session on 27 May 1967 at the Denver Museum of Natural History where, surrounded by neolithic and paleolithic artefacts, it was hoped his powers might capture on film something that was several thousand years old.

Serios felt confident of success and began by drawing a mental impression he had received of a man lighting a fire. Strange images were recorded on several of the

Hidden in the hand?

James Randi, professional stage magician and debunker of things paranormal, is convinced that Ted Serios is a fraud and that his so-called 'thoughtographs' are produced not by the power of his mind but by the device Serios calls a 'gismo'.

A 'typical Serios gimmick', described by Randi in his book *Flim-flam! – the truth about unicorns, parapsychology and other delusions*, consists of a small magnifying lens, about ½ inch (1.2 centimetres) in diameter and with a focal length of about 1½ inches (4 centimetres), fixed to one end of a cylinder about 1½ inches (4 centimetres) long. A circle cut from a colour transparency (a 35-millimetre slide, for example) is glued to the other end of the cylinder. To avoid detection,

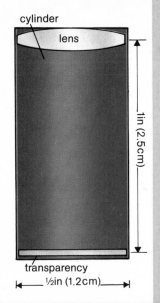

cylinder
lens
1in (2.5cm)
transparency
½in (1.2cm)

the device can be wrapped loosely in a tube of paper.

By holding the 'gismo' – lens end towards the palm – close to the lens of a Polaroid camera focused to infinity, and snapping the shutter, the image on the transparency will be thrown onto the Polaroid film. After use, Randi explains, the 'gismo' will slide easily out of the paper (to be disposed of secretly later) and the empty paper tube can be offered for inspection.

It is possible to take photographs in this way, although the pictures that result will usually be of poor quality, just as those 'taken' by Serios were. However, showing how the images *could* have been produced is very different from using such an optical device undetected in hundreds of demonstrations. And neither Randi nor any other of Ted Serios's critics has done that.

pictures, the most impressive of which shows a Neanderthal man in a crouching position. But Serios's camera lens had *not* delved into time to record this image. It was realised immediately by one witness, Professor H. Marie Wormington, of the Department of Anthropology, Colorado College, that it resembled very closely a well-known life-size model of a Neanderthal man group in the Chicago Field Museum of Natural History, postcards of which were readily available.

The final curtain

So, was Serios faking the photographs? Subsequent studies show that the man in Serios's pictures is shown at different angles and in the opinion of several professional photographers and photogrammetric engineers, these paranormal prints 'could not have been produced from a single microtransparency, but would have required at least several and perhaps eight different ones, most of which could not have been produced from a simple photographic copying of the Field Museum photograph or of a photograph taken by Ted himself.'

Soon after this session, Serios's psychic powers waned and within a year, although he continued to submit to experiments, all he could produce were 'blackies' or 'whities' without discernible images, leaving psychical researchers still baffled about just what paranormal forces had been at work to produce his astonishing pictures.

Serios had lost his powers at other times – the longest period being for two years – and it seemed to happen without warning. He said: 'It is as if a curtain comes down, ker-boom, and that's all, brother.'

But perhaps there was a warning. The last supervised full-frame thoughtograph he produced was in June 1967 . . . and it showed the image of a curtain.

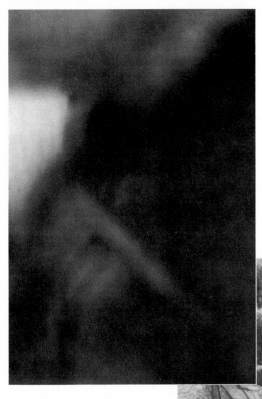

Left: Serios's version of a life-size model of a group of Neanderthals in the Field Museum of Natural History in Chicago (below)

The hidden face c

One of the strangest stories to have emerged from the cloud of mystery that surrounds the ancient science of alchemy is that of the modern master Fulcanelli. KENNETH RAYNER JOHNSON describes what is known of this extraordinary man

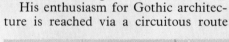

THE NAME FULCANELLI has flickered tantalisingly in and out of modern occult literature and speculation for more than half a century. Yet the identity of the 20th-century alchemist behind the pseudonym remains a complete mystery.

Today, Fulcanelli has taken on the aura almost of an alchemical 'saint' – an ageless adept of our own times, as enigmatic and fascinating as the semi-legendary Comte de St Germain.

It was in the early 1920s that the Fulcanelli legend started: Parisian occultists and alchemists began overhearing oblique and intriguing references to an actual master, alive and working secretly in their midst. These came mainly from Eugène Canseliet, an intense, slightly-built man in his early twenties who was known to be an enthusiastic researcher into alchemy. They were also bandied about by his constant companion and friend, an impoverished artist and illustrator, Jean-Julien Champagne, who was 22 years Canseliet's senior. The pair, who rented adjacent quarters on the sixth storey of a dilapidated tenement at 59 bis, rue de Rochechouart, in the Butte-Montmartre district, quickly became the focal point of a small, select circle of occultists. They were frequently seen in the city's great libraries, the Arsenal, the Sainte Geneviève, the Mazarin and the Bibliothèque Nationale, poring over rare books and manuscripts.

Those on the periphery of this informal study-group heard hints that 'the Master, Fulcanelli' was elderly, distinguished, rich, immensely learned and possibly even of aristocratic or noble lineage. He was a genuine, practising alchemist who, if he had not done so already, was on the brink of perfecting the Great Work – the manufacture of the Philosopher's Stone, which would ennoble base metals to perfection by transmutation, and the Elixir, which could prolong life indefinitely.

But who the Master really was remained a mystery. Few had apparently actually met him – except, so they claimed, Champagne and Canseliet. Sceptics began to question the fact of his existence.

Then, in the autumn of 1926, evidence of the Master's reality – or at least the reality of someone – appeared. It came in the form of a remarkable book, *Le mystère des cathédrales* ('The mystery of the cathedrals'), published in a limited luxury edition of only 300 copies, by Jean Schemit, of 45 rue Lafitte, in the Opéra district. It was subtitled 'An esoteric

The mystery of the cathedrals

In his book *Le mystère des cathédrales* Fulcanelli takes the reader on a guided and interpretative tour of many of France's finest examples of Gothic architecture, including the Cathedral of Notre Dame in Paris (below). Like many mystical commentators before him, he sees architecture as a means of passing on esoteric knowledge, encoded in the form and proportion of the building, its sculpture and stained glass.

His enthusiasm for Gothic architecture is reached via a circuitous route

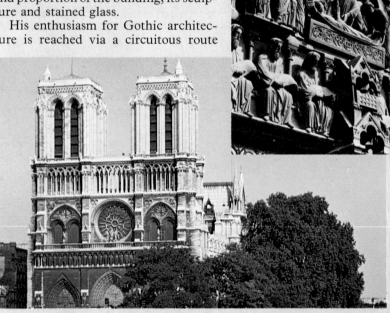

ulcanelli

The Greek Sun-god Helios in his chariot, in a detail from a vase, and the Roman fire-god Vulcan, in a relief found at the Roman camp of Corstopitum in Northumbria. 'Fulcanelli' is a phonetic approximation of 'Vulcan' and 'Helios' – an allusion, perhaps, to the flames used to heat the mysterious substances that combine to form the Elixir of Life

Opposite page: this bracket in the mansion of Lallemant in Bourges shows a medieval adept holding the Vessel of the Great Work, in which the Elixir of Life is prepared

Above left: 59 bis, rue de Rochechouart, Paris. In this house lived Eugène Canseliet and Jean-Julien Champagne, reputedly pupils of the mysterious Fulcanelli

Below: Marguerite de France (1553–1615), who perhaps knew the secret of the Great Work. Rumour suggested Fulcanelli might be descended from her

involving a kind of punning logic. He interprets gothic art, *art gothique*, as *argot*-hique – and, he says, *argot* (cant or slang) is defined in dictionaries as 'a language peculiar to all individuals who wish to communicate their thoughts without being understood by outsiders.' And he claims that those who use this secret language are descendants of the sailors who accompanied Jason on his search for the Golden Fleece – aboard the ship *Argo*; they, he claims, 'spoke the *langue argotique* [language of the Argo] . . . while they were sailing towards the felicitous shores of Colchos . . .'

How does Fulcanelli's method work in practice? In the Portal of the Virgin of Notre Dame Cathedral (left), he sees the medallions of the sarcophagus as symbols of the seven planetary metals. (In the standard alchemical interpretation, the Sun stands for gold, Mercury for quicksilver, Saturn for lead, Venus for copper, the Moon for silver, Jupiter for tin and Mars for iron.) Taken as a whole, Fulcanelli claims, the portal gives clues as to how to transmute these metals. But Fulcanelli has not made matters too easy; the final step in interpretation is left to the alchemist. Perhaps this is just as well – for, as Fulcanelli's pupil Canseliet reveals in his introduction to the book, the '*key to the major arcanum* is given quite openly in one of the figures.'

interpretation of the hermetic symbols of the Great Work'. Its preface was by Eugène Canseliet, then aged only 26, and it contained 36 illustrations, two in colour, by the artist Champagne. The text itself was ascribed simply to Fulcanelli.

It purported to interpret the symbolism of various Gothic cathedrals and other buildings in Europe as encoded instructions of alchemical secrets, a concept only darkly hinted at by previous writers on the esoteric in art and architecture. Among occultists, it caused a minor sensation.

But even in his original preface, the young Canseliet intimated that his Master, Fulcanelli – the name is a phonetic approximation of Vulcan, the blacksmith god, and Helios, the sun-charioteer – had attained the Stone, become mystically transfigured and illuminated, and had disappeared.

He disappeared when the fatal hour struck, when the Sign was accomplished. . . . Fulcanelli is no more. But we have at least this consolation that his thought remains, warm and vital, enshrined for ever in these pages.

Perhaps understandably – especially in view of the immense scholarship and unique haunting qualities of the book – speculation about Fulcanelli's true identity ran wild within the occult fraternity.

There were suggestions that he was a surviving member of the former French royal family, the Valois. Although they were supposed to have died out in 1589 upon the demise of Henri III, it was known that members of the family had dabbled in magic and mysticism and that Marguerite de France, daughter of Henri II and wife of Henri IV of Navarre, survived until 1615. What is more, one of her many lovers was the esoterically inclined Francis Bacon (whom many still claim as an adept to this day); she was divorced in 1599 and her personal crest bore the magical pentagram, each of whose five points carried one letter of the Latin word *salus* – meaning 'health'. Could the reputedly aristocratic Fulcanelli be a descendant of the Valois, and did the Latin motto hint that some important alchemical secret of longevity had been passed on to him by the family? It was, at least, one possibility.

There were other, more or less plausible identifications. Some claimed Fulcanelli was a bookseller-occultist, Pierre Dujols, who with his wife ran a shop in the rue de Rennes in the Luxembourg district of Paris. But Dujols was already known to have been only a speculative alchemist, writing under the nom de plume of Magophon. Why should he hide behind two aliases? Another suggestion was that Fulcanelli was the writer J.H. Rosny the elder. Yet his life was too well-known to the public for this theory to find acceptance.

There were also at least three practical alchemists working in the city around the same period. They operated under the respective pseudonymns of Auriger, Faugerons and Dr Jaubert. The argument against them being Fulcanelli was much the same as that against Dujols-Magophon: why use more than one alias?

Finally, there were Eugène Canseliet and Jean-Julien Champagne, both of whom were directly connected with Fulcanelli's book, and both of whom had claimed to have known the Master personally.

The argument against Canseliet's identification as the Master was fairly straightforward: he was far too young to have acquired the erudition and knowledge so obviously and remarkably demonstrated by the text of *Le mystère des cathédrales*. And a study of his preface showed a distinct difference in style from that of the text, a difference that remains notable in Canseliet's more recent writings.

Champagne, meanwhile, seemed to some the more likely contender. He was older and more experienced, and his work as an artist

Above: Eugène Canseliet, pupil of Fulcanelli, who continues to keep the secret of the master alchemist's identity

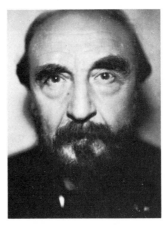

Above: the writer J. H. Rosny the elder (1856–1940) who, many people suspected, was the figure behind the pseudonym 'Fulcanelli'

Left: Jean-Julien Champagne, artist and illustrator, and constant companion of Fulcanelli's pupil Eugène Canseliet. Champagne was a braggart and a practical joker, and his habit of trying to pass himself off as Fulcanelli added to the confusion about the true identity of the master alchemist

could have taken him around the various cathedrals, châteaux and other curious monuments whose symbolism Fulcanelli had obviously studied and interpreted in great detail as keys to the Great Work.

On the other hand, Champagne was a noted braggart, practical joker, punster and drunkard, who frequently liked to pass himself off as Fulcanelli – although his behaviour was entirely out of keeping with the traditional solemn oath of the adept to remain anonymous and let his written work speak for itself.

A vain and dangerous quest

Two examples of Champagne's wicked sense of humour suffice to show the great gap between his own way of thinking and that of the noble-minded author of *Le mystère des cathédrales*. Champagne once persuaded a gullible young follower that he should stock up a massive supply of coal to ensure that his alchemical furnace was kept constantly burning at the required temperature. The naïve youth lugged sack after sack of the fuel up to his garret until there was barely room in which to lie down and sleep. Champagne then announced to the would-be alchemist that the quest was an utterly vain and dangerous one – leaving him almost banished from his apartment by coal and, presumably, considerably out of pocket into the bargain.

The other carefully contrived prank of Champagne involved his forging a letter, purportedly from Monsieur Paul le Cour, who edited and published a periodical called *Atlantis*, to the publisher of the *Mercure de France*. In it, the fake le Cour urged the setting up of a fund by the *Mercure*'s subscribers to build a monument for the victims of the fabled lost continent – a cenotaph that, since he suggested it be placed in the Sargasso Sea, would have to be unsinkable. Champagne sat back and laughed while the unsuspecting 'real' le Cour received an indignant volley from the *Mercure* publisher.

To crown all of this, Champagne's huge

appetite for absinthe and Pernod finally killed him. He died in 1932 of gangrene in his sixth-floor garret. His friend Canseliet nursed him through his long, painful and particularly unpleasant illness (Champagne's toes actually fell off). The poor artist was aged only 55.

Only three years earlier, a second work by the mysterious Fulcanelli had been published, again by Jean Schemit. It was *Les demeures philosophales* ('The dwellings of the philosophers'), which was in two volumes and double the length of the first book. Like its predecessor, it interpreted particular architectural embellishments, such as ornate ceiling panels – this time in 12th- to 15th-century mansions and châteaux – as encoded alchemical knowledge.

The appearance of this book inspired yet another theory about Fulcanelli's possible

Below: F. Jolivet Castelot, a practising 'archimist' – someone who tries to use ordinary chemical methods to transmute base metals into gold – and yet another Fulcanelli-suspect

identity. Inside the rear cover of the second volume were the armorial bearings of Dom Robert Jollivet, a 13th-century abbot of Mont-St-Michel, known to have dabbled in alchemy. This, according to the theory, implied that the name of Jollivet was intended to indicate that his modern near-namesake, F. Jolivet Castelot, was in fact Fulcanelli. Jolivet Castelot was President of the Alchemists' Society of France from around 1914 and was a member of the Ordre Kabbalistique de la Rose-Croix. Between 1896 and 1935, he had published many studies in hermeticism, alchemy and spa-gyrics – the art of making chemical/medical preparations using alchemical principles. But he made no secret of the fact that he was an 'archimist' rather than an alchemist – that is, a researcher who tried to effect transmutation by orthodox chemistry, rather than a more mystically inclined alchemist.

There was, however, an even stranger heraldic shield on the final page of the original edition of *Le mystère des cathédrales*. The occult scholar Robert Ambelain who,

Is this inscription on the grave of Jean-Julien Champagne, containing clues pointing to Fulcanelli, merely a last attempt to convince people he was the mysterious alchemist?

in the 1930s, made one of the most thorough investigations into the Fulcanelli mystery was the first to draw attention to this shield. Among many other alleged clues, Ambelain pointed out that the dog-Latin motto beneath the shield was *uber campa agna*, which was a phonetic approximation of Hubert Champagne. And, he claimed, Hubert was the middle name of the artist, Jean-Julien Champagne, He also noted that the pseudonym Fulcanelli is an anagram of *l'écu finale* ('the final shield'), thus indirectly indicating the heraldic device and its motto.

Eugène Canseliet, however, has flatly denied the identification of Champagne as Fulcanelli – or of anyone else, for that matter – consistently since 1926. Hubert was not the artist's middle name, he claims – although it is, by sheer coincidence, that of his own maternal grandfather. In any case, he further asserts, the damning shield was inserted into the first edition of the book by Champagne – without the permission or knowledge of the Master, Fulcanelli, or of himself – another practical joke!

Deceptions and forgeries

Canseliet, who is Fulcanelli's sole surviving pupil and official literary executor, similarly claims that an inscription on Champagne's gravestone, along with a deliberate forgery of Fulcanelli's signature by the artist, were further attempts to deceive or mislead. The gravestone epitaph, at the cemetery of Arnouvilles-les-Gonesses, reads:

Here rests Jean-Julien Champagne
Apostolicus Hermeticae Scientiae
1877–1932

The alleged Fulcanelli signature, meanwhile, appeared in a handwritten dedication of the original edition of *Le mystère des cathédrales*, given by Champagne to an occultist named Jules Boucher. It was signed A.H.S. Fulcanelli – the same initials as those of the Latin motto on the gravestone. And in Jules Boucher's *Manual of magic*, the author's dedication is to 'my master Fulcanelli'.

Curiously enough, despite all his alleged evidence to the contrary, Ambelain reaches the conclusion that Champagne did actually achieve the Philosopher's Stone – the stone that transmutes base metals into gold and allows the manufacture of the Elixir of Life – some three years before his death.

But if Ambelain is correct, how could this explain Champagne's untimely and less than dignified death through over-indulgence in drink at the age of 55? Quite simply, it doesn't make sense.

And yet, more than one person has attested to Fulcanelli's success in transmutation and to his continued existence – even in the 1980s – which would make him more than 130 years old!

Transformation of an alchemist

At their final meeting in 1954, Canseliet reported that his master Fulcanelli seemed youthful – although he must have been over 100 years old. Had he found the secret of eternal life?

IN FRANCE THE NAME of Fulcanelli quickly found popular acceptance as the traditional pseudonym of an alchemical Master. Go to the 16th-century Château de Terre-Neuve, Vendée, even today, and there you will be shown an ornately decorated 'alchemical fireplace' – and the French guide will tell you it is the one of which Fulcanelli wrote in *Les demeures philosophales*, without even bothering to explain who Fulcanelli was . . . or is.

But to English-speaking students of occultism and alchemy, it was not until 1963 that the publication of Louis Pauwels's and Jacques Bergier's best-seller *The dawn of magic* in English ensured that Fulcanelli and his works came to be more widely known. And it was a further eight years before Fulcanelli's first masterpiece, *Le mystère des cathédrales*, was translated into English.

Each of these books provided astounding new information about Fulcanelli. The latter, for example, contained the bold assertion by Fulcanelli's disciple Eugène Canseliet that the Master had given him a minute quantity of the alchemical 'powder of projection' in 1922 – and permitted him to transmute 4 ounces (100 grams) of lead into gold. The experiment, Canseliet told Walter

Below: the noted French atomic physicist André Helbronner. In 1937 his research assistant Jacques Bergier was warned of the implications of manipulating nuclear energy by a mysterious stranger – whom he identified as Fulcanelli

Lang, who wrote the book's introduction, took place in the unlikely setting of a gasworks at Sarcelles before two witnesses: the artist Jean-Julien Champagne and a young chemist named Gaston Sauvage.

Furthermore, in a letter to Lang, Canseliet maintained that, when he had last worked with Fulcanelli, 'The Master was already a very old man but he carried his eighty years lightly. Thirty years later, I was to see him again . . . and he appeared to be a man of fifty. That is to say, he appeared to be no older than I was myself.'

Canseliet, aged 80 in 1981, has subsequently asserted that he has, on more than one occasion, kept a secret rendezvous with his Master – and that Fulcanelli is still very much alive.

Another possible appearance of the Master was reported by Pauwels and Bergier in their book. Bergier claimed that in June 1937 – eight years before the first atom-bomb test in New Mexico – he was approached by an impressive but mysterious stranger. The man asked Bergier to pass on a message to the noted physicist André Helbronner, for whom he was then working. He said he felt it his duty to warn orthodox scientists, now

Louis Pauwels (right) and Jacques Bergier (far right), whose best-selling *The dawn of magic*, published in 1963, brought the first news of Fulcanelli to English-speaking readers

that they were on the brink of being able to manipulate nuclear energy, of the danger of this new discovery. The alchemists of bygone times – and previous civilisations that had destroyed themselves – had obtained such secret knowledge. The stranger said he held out no hope that his warning would be heeded, but nonetheless felt obliged to issue it. Bergier remained convinced, right up to his death in November 1978, that the enigmatic stranger was Fulcanelli.

As a result of Bergier's experience, the American Office for Strategic Services, forerunner of the CIA, made a search for Fulcanelli when the Second World War ended in 1945. They were anxious to round up anyone who had prior knowledge of nuclear physics, to prevent their defection to hostile powers. But Fulcanelli could not be found.

Alchemy and the atom bomb

There is, however, one flaw in Bergier's story. According to his own account, the man who visited him, while speaking apparently knowledgeably about the manipulation of nuclear energy, mentioned the element plutonium. Yet this element was not isolated until February 1941, by the physicist Glenn T. Seaborg, at Berkeley, California. Furthermore, it was not actually *named* plutonium until March 1942 – five years after Bergier's alleged encounter. In fact, Element 94, as it was previously called, was almost dubbed 'plutium' – but Seaborg, as its discoverer, decided plutonium rolled more easily off the tongue.

But the fact remains that Bergier claimed that *someone* highly knowledgeable visited him at the Paris Gas Board laboratory in 1937. And he was said to have a photographic memory.

There is one further account that tells of a transmutation performed by Fulcanelli himself. It comes from a modern alchemist, now

Glenn T. Seaborg, who discovered the element plutonium in 1941. Bergier claimed that the stranger who visited him in 1937 mentioned plutonium by name – and yet this event occurred four years before the element was isolated, and five years before it was actually called plutonium

operating from Salt Lake City, Utah. He is Frater Albertus Spagyricus, born Albert Riedel in Dresden, Germany, in 1911. A former interior decorator, Frater Albertus now heads the flourishing Paracelsus College (Utah Institute of Parachemistry), formed originally as the Paracelsus Research Society in 1960. The college operates regular seminars on alchemical subjects at its headquarters and seeks to 'bring alchemy out of the Dark Ages'.

In his book *The alchemist of the Rocky Mountains* (1975), Frater Albertus claims that Fulcanelli transmuted half a pound (200 grams) of lead into gold and 4 ounces (100 grams) of silver into uranium in 1937 – the same year, it will be noted, as Bergier's meeting with the mysterious stranger. The experiment, according to Albertus, took place at the Castel de Leré, near Bourges, and was witnessed by the castle's owner, Pierre de Lesseps, along with two unnamed physicists, a chemist and geologist.

When Fulcanelli added an 'unknown substance' to the half-pound of molten lead, says Albertus, it was transmuted into the same weight in gold. Afterwards, Fulcanelli did the same with the silver, producing a like amount of uranium.

Asked what the unknown substance was, Fulcanelli 'would only mention offhandedly that it was derived from ferrous pyrite (fool's gold), a ferrous sulphide FeS_2.'

The present author wrote to Frater Albertus asking for his sources of information. But an assistant politely answered that Frater Albertus was unfortunately too busy teaching and attending to his lecture programme to be able to answer personally and in detail.

According to Frater Albertus, however, it was after the 1937 transmutation that Fulcanelli disappeared.

The only other person who has claimed to have contacted Fulcanelli in more recent

The perfect being

The aim of alchemists in attempting to complete the Great Work is not merely to enable them to change base metals into gold, or even to achieve eternal youth. For alchemists believe that every stage in the alchemical process is accompanied by a spiritual change in the person conducting the work.

The secret of the alchemical art is said to be contained in the aphoristic principle *solve et coagula*, 'dissolve and combine'. This is a fair description of the physical aspect of the alchemical process: at each stage, the various characteristics of a substance are stripped away, and a new, nobler substance is built up. In the spiritual aspect, this means a 'death' followed by a 'rebirth' into a better, purer life – a concept familiar in many religions; St Paul, for instance, exhorts the faithful to 'die to sin and live to righteousness'.

In the final stage of the Great Work, 'the King is reunited in the Fire of Love with his blessed Queen' – and the Alchemist becomes the perfect being, the Divine Androgyne, the perfect conjunction of man and woman.

times is his faithful pupil Canseliet. He has asserted that he met his Master in Spain in 1954 in highly unusual circumstances.

If Fulcanelli was, as Canseliet maintains, 80 when last they worked together in the late 1920s, it would make the Master Alchemist between 100 and 110 years old by the time of the Spanish meeting. Confirmation that Canseliet did indeed go to Spain that year was obtained by the late Gerard Heym, founder member of the Society for the Study of Alchemy and Early Chemistry and editor of *Ambix*, its journal. Heym, who was acclaimed by many as Europe's foremost occult scholar of his day, made friends with Canseliet's daughter and through her managed to take a look at his passport. It carried a Spanish entry-visa stamp for 1954.

But how Canseliet received the summons to Spain and what actually went on there is highly mysterious. Heym told the occultist Walter Lang that he gained the impression that a message was received in some paranormal way, possibly through clairvoyance. And a close friend of Canseliet, who was still engaged in alchemical research in 1981 and must remain anonymous, told the present writer: 'He has told me in detail how he met Fulcanelli in Spain – in another dimension, as it were, or rather at a point where such meetings are possible.'

Further enquiries elicited the information that Canseliet went to Seville and was met and taken by a long, circuitous route to a large mountain château. It turned out to be a secret colony of alchemists – and it was here that Canseliet had once again met his former

Frater Albertus Spagyricus, director of Paracelsus College, the Utah Institute of Parachemistry. He claims that in 1937, before three witnesses, Fulcanelli performed transmutations of lead into gold, and silver into uranium

Master in such mysterious circumstances.

But, even more peculiar to those not familiar with alchemical philosophy and its aura of mysticism, Fulcanelli appeared to have undergone a curious form of transformation. He seemed androgynous – to have characteristics of both men and women.

Canseliet has told sources close to him – he does not receive casual visitors and cannot deal with his massive mail – that Fulcanelli actually had the appearance of a woman. This kind of physical change has been reported in obscure pockets of alchemical literature as one of the side effects of taking the Elixir of Life. If the elixir is successful, the subject is said to lose all his hair, teeth and nails, then regrow them and take on younger, smoother, almost asexual facial features.

According to Gerard Heym, Canseliet returned home with only vague recollections of his experiences in Spain – almost as if, said Heym, he had been subjected to some form of hypnosis, designed to make him forget the details of what he had seen and been told.

Curiously enough, Canseliet has admitted his own failure to perfect the Third Degree of the Great Work – the manufacture of the Stone and Elixir. And, apart from being a respected author and savant on the alchemical art, he seems to have gained little personal benefit – financially or otherwise – from his long association with the mysterious Fulcanelli.

The image of perfection

Alchemists believe that, in the final stage of the Great Work, the adept himself is transformed into a 'perfect being' – half man, half woman.

ON HIS MYSTERIOUS VISIT to Spain in 1954, Eugène Canseliet claimed he again saw his Master, Fulcanelli – transfigured, as it seemed, by the results of his alchemical attainment. The Master appeared not only to have retrieved his youth and vitality, but was clear-skinned and effeminate – perhaps even, Canseliet said, asexual.

Absurd as this idea may sound, especially to those unversed in alchemical philosophy, there is within the deeper esoteric traditions of the Hermetic art a suggestion that with the blinding flash of illumination that heralds success comes a tremendous change in the adept, both spiritual and physical. Like the base metal that attainment of the Philosopher's Stone permits him to transmute into gold, the alchemist himself is transformed utterly. The metamorphosed adept takes the form of a perfect balance of the female and male polarities within human nature – and with it, an outward form of bisexuality or hermaphroditism, certainly in the facial features. These mysterious changes, the results of inner, profound, spiritual experiences – with equally physical, tangible effects – have been said to occur also in saints, holy men and devotional mystics in beatific states.

Could the modern alchemist Fulcanelli have undergone this transformation after attaining the Stone and Elixir and completing the Great Work?

In his second book, *Les demeures philosophales*, Fulcanelli indicates that he is not unaware of this possibility. In fact, he draws particular attention to a remarkable piece of sculpture – one of four statues that guard the tomb of François II in Nantes Cathedral. Fulcanelli calls it Prudence.

In frontal view, it depicts the figure of a beautiful young girl in a hooded cloak and floor-length gown. She seems mesmerised by her own reflection in a strange, convex mirror she holds in her left hand. In her right hand is a set of compasses – or perhaps *dividers*; throughout alchemical literature, there are frequent injunctions to separate and conjoin. And on the back of the girl's head is another face – that of a full-bearded, wise old sage, apparently deep in philosophical contemplation.

Fulcanelli compares this figure of Prudence with the god Janus, the two-faced, son of Apollo and Creusa. Enfolded within the cloak of philosophy, he says, she symbolises nature in all her aspects – both inward and outward. But beneath her exterior veil, he adds, there appears the mysterious image of ancient alchemy, 'and we are, through the attributes of the first, initiated into the secrets of the second.' He writes:

It is generally recommended to unite

A statue representing Prudence, from the tomb of François II in Nantes Cathedral. It shows the figure of a young girl – with the face of a wise old man on the back of her head. Fulcanelli believed the statue symbolised nature in all her aspects, and also the final stage of the alchemical process, in which opposites combine to produce the perfect, androgynous, being

A cryptic message

The penultimate chapter of Fulcanelli's book *Le mystère des cathédrales* concerns an unusual stone cross located in the village of Hendaye in the foothills of the Pyrenees. Somewhat circumspectly, Fulcanelli suggests that the monument contains encoded prophecies indicating a future cataclysm.

Fulcanelli believes that the inscription INRI, normally rendered as *Iesus Nazarenus Rex Iudeorum* ('Jesus of Nazareth, King of the Jews'), has a second

interpretation that gives the cross its true meaning: *Igne Natura Renovatur Integra*, 'by fire nature is renewed whole'. This, Fulcanelli claims, is a reference to the purifying fire that will soon consume the northern hemisphere.

He also draws attention to the strange inscription OCRUXAVES PESUNICA at the head of the cross. This can be broken up to form the phrase *O crux ave spes unica*, 'Hail, o cross, the only hope'. But the strange way in which the inscription is carved suggests that there may be a hidden message.

By an extension of what Fulcanelli calls the phonetic cabala, a retired engineer and student of Fulcanelli's cryptographic writings, Paul Mevry, has arrived at a fascinating new interpretation. OCRUXAVES PESUNICA is an anagram of the Latin phrase *Orcus ave pus e canis*, meaning 'Orcus, hail, down from the Dog'. Orcus is the Roman Lord of the Underworld – whom the ancient Egyptians knew as Osiris, the Lord of the Dead. Since the Egyptians associated Osiris with the Dog star, Sirius, could this then be some form of warning of destruction to come from the system of Sirius and its dark companion Sirius B?

And could the very location of the cross at Hendaye – similar to *end-day* – be a clue to the coming apocalypse?

'an old man, hale and vigorous, with a young and beautiful virgin.' Of these alchemical nuptials, a metallic child is born and receives the epithet of *androgyne*, because he possesses all at once the nature of sulphur, his father, and that of his mother, mercury . . . . Practically all esoteric systems of self-illumination, of raising the base human body and spirit to a higher state, at some stage emphasise the necessity – allegorically or otherwise – to attain this inner balance of the

male and female polarities. And the concept even squares with more modern psychoanalytic thinking, especially with Jungian psychology. Indeed, Jung himself devoted more than 10 years of his life to the study of alchemy and wrote several large volumes on the subject, linking its strange 'archetypal' symbolism to that of dreams, inner experiences – and psychology.

The symbolism of the Divine Androgyne is not, by any means, simply physical or sexual. Its main, inner meaning appears to

The tangled web

'The picture of the labyrinth,' Fulcanelli tells us in *Le mystère des cathédrales*, is 'emblematic of the whole labour of the Work. . . . It is there that the *thread of Ariadne* becomes necessary for him [the alchemist] if he is not to wander among the winding paths of the task, unable to extricate himself.'

He goes on to use the phonetic cabala to elucidate the symbolic value of the famous Greek legend of Ariadne, who with a thread helped Theseus to escape after he had slain the Minotaur.

'Ariane (Ariadne) is a form of *airagne*

(araignée, the spider). . . . In Spanish ñ is pronounced gn; αράχνη [pronounced arachne] (the spider) can thus be read *arahne, arahni, arahagne*. Is not our soul the spider, which weaves our own body? . . . The verb αἴρω [airo] means *to take, to seize, to draw, to attract*; whence αἴρην [airen], that which takes, seizes, attracts. Thus αἴρην is the lodestone, that virtue shut up in the body. . . .'

Fulcanelli connects, through some cunning twists of logic, the Provençal *aran, iran, airan* – iron – with the Greek αρυαν meaning both 'lodestone' and 'rising sun'. And there he leaves it – a set of tantalising word-associations, significant only for the initiated.

or, as he confided to one associate 'in another dimension, as it were'? It is mere conjecture, of course, but could he have been the subject of some form of initiation into the deeper mysteries of the Hermetic Quest? In the light of alchemical tradition, there would seem to be no other logical explanation for Canseliet's bizarre encounter.

And why should an elderly man, respected for decades as an authority on alchemy, invent such a weird and wonderful tale – at the risk of his reputation?

No one has managed to identify the historical person who hid behind the cloaked pseudonym of Fulcanelli. And M. Canseliet, if he *does* know the personality behind that name, has certainly respected the anonymity of his most unusual and erudite Master.

evoke stability, harmony, perfect balance in all possible ways. In the system of the Jewish *qabalah*, this finds beautiful religious expression in several passages of the Lesser Holy Assembly: 'When the Bride is united to the King in the excellence of the Sabbath, then are all things made one body,' and 'the beauty of the female is completed by the beauty of the male. . . . When the Mother is united to the King, the worlds receive a blessing and are found in the joy of the universe.'

How may these concepts be equated with the strange experience of Canseliet in Spain –

Above left: a Roman coin showing the two faces of Janus, Roman god of doors and archways, sometimes referred to as *divom deus*, the god of gods

Below: in the Lallement house in Bourges is a *bas-relief* of the Golden Fleece (right). Fulcanelli claimed the story was 'a complete representation of the hermetic process'

The strange histories of Joan Grant

Have we all had previous existences in many different centuries and civilisations? Joan Grant believes she has – and ROY STEMMAN recounts the fascinating story of how she has learned to trace those many other lives

JOAN GRANT HIT the public eye in 1937 with her first highly praised book, *Winged pharaoh*. It was classified as an historical novel and, like others that followed, was judged by the experts to be a very accurate account of the time it portrayed. But Joan Grant did not have to research a single detail – she recorded everything from her 'far memory' of the life she had lived as a priest-pharaoh in a previous incarnation.

Joan Grant had intimations of her other lives even as a tiny child; she told stories about who she had been 'before she was Joan' – but nobody believed her. Soon she learned that it was better to keep her stories to herself, and she told nobody else until she was a teenager. Meanwhile, she struggled to unravel her strange dreams and to understand who she was. It took a great effort to train herself to wake several times a night so she could write down the events that had just occurred in her sleep.

Joan Grant was born in 1907 of a wealthy family and lived a sheltered life of comfort and plenty. Even during the First World War she suffered little physical privation. But during that time she began to have vivid

Joan Grant, flanked by her first and best-known book and a photograph of herself as a girl. She had glimpses of other lives even as a tiny child – and Winged pharaoh told the story of one of them as a priest-ruler in ancient Egypt

war dreams in which all five senses were engaged. In fact, the smells of battlefield and hospital made her violently sick upon waking, and for weeks she tried to keep herself from sleeping by self-torture such as sitting on an icy floor or pulling hairs out. At one point during this time, when at a convent in London where she loved the nuns, she was constantly terrified for no reason. Nearly 20 years later she found out that the reason lay in a life she had lived in the 16th century.

One morning at home she came down late for breakfast after a terrible nightmare. There was a soldier with her father, and Joan said to him:

Somehow I know you will not laugh at me. Last night I was with a man called McAndrew when he was killed. I can describe the regimental badge although I cannot remember the name of the regiment, except that it was not an English one. And I can tell you the slang name of his trench.

The visitor did not laugh because he was able to identify the regiment as Canadian. Later, he wrote to Joan's father, Jack Marshall:

For heaven's sake don't laugh at the

child. I cannot attempt an explanation, but I have checked what she said. A battalion of that regiment went over the top on a night attack a few hours before she told me about it at breakfast. A private called McAndrew was among the killed. She was even correct about the local name of the front-line trench. Joan was only nine at the time, and it was years before her father told her of this unexpected confirmation.

Marshall was a scientist who won a CBE for his work in mosquito research, on which he wrote the standard text. Many eminent men were visitors to his home. One, C.G. Lamb, was professor of engineering at Cambridge University and Joan's special favourite. They had long talks and she felt at ease with him, partly because of his great interest in psychical research.

Lamb had been a friend of Joan's grandmother, Jennie Marshall. One day while they were chatting, he told Joan that Jennie could have been a world-famous concert pianist if her husband had not stood in her way. 'Jennie gives me music lessons,' said Joan in reply, aware that any other adult would have scoffed at the claim, since Jennie was dead. 'Father knows I would never be a first-class pianist so there is no point in my having lessons, but Jennie knows I need music and she teaches me. Sometimes she plays the piano with me – music that is quite different from the ordinary tunes I have learned.'

Feeling that her grandmother was present, young Joan went to the piano and music began to flow. When she stopped, Lamb mopped his brow and remarked: 'Extraordinary. Quite extraordinary but completely evidential. What you have just played was

Top: Seacourt, the childhood home of Joan Grant at Hayling in Hampshire

Above: C.G. Lamb, professor of engineering at Cambridge University, was interested in psychical research and gave a sympathetic ear to Joan Grant's accounts of unusual occurrences. And in one instance he was able to prove from personal knowledge that her experience was paranormal

Left: Blanche and Jack Marshall, parents of Joan Grant. Through her father's wide social contacts, Joan met H.G. Wells. The author advised her to keep her 'secret life' to herself for a while – and then to write about it later

often played to me by your grandmother. . . . I have not heard it since she died.'

When Joan suggested that she may have heard her grandmother play it, or have heard it at a concert, Lamb assured her that she had not.

Only one copy of that music ever existed. It was given in manuscript to the Tsar of Russia, who sent it to your grandmother. . . . I happen to know that the manuscript of that music, together with several other manuscripts of similar value, was burned two years before you were born.

Jennie Marshall had learned that she had terminal cancer, and decided that no one else would play her music if she could not do so.

It was to the author H.G. Wells, whom she met at the age of 16, that Joan confessed all about 'the secret part of her life'. He was sympathetic, but advised her to keep it to herself until she was 'strong enough to bear being laughed at by fools'; then, when she was ready, she should write down what she knew – 'It is important that you become a writer,' said Wells.

Joan Grant broke off her first engagement because her fiancé and his family were intolerant of her belief in her dream lives. It was indeed a dream that led her to her next romance.

This dream of a man recurred over a period of time, during which she went to Switzerland for a ski-ing holiday. Alone in the hotel music room, she was playing Jennie's music on the piano when the door opened – and she looked into the eyes of the man in her dream. The stranger looked at her intently and then said, 'It really is you. I have dreamed with you for nearly two years':

dictation. Joan says she learned how to shift levels of consciousness between sleep and wakefulness so that she did not have to break the thread of events and was able to describe her dreams as she had them. This, she said, helped her to dip more easily into what she called her 'far memory'. Her far-memory dreams transcended space and time.

Another category of her dreams she called 'true dreams'. These depicted incidents that were later found to have occurred at about the time she was dreaming. In one such dream she was a sailor on a burning ship. On waking she told Leslie about it. There was enough detail to say with certainty that the ship was in the Channel, the sailor was French, and the vessel was going to Cherbourg. She thought the ship's name was *Atlantic*. Later that day, newspaper headlines declared '*Atlantique* burns in English Channel: many dead'.

Besides far-memory dreams, Joan Grant soon discovered another way of tuning into the past. At her husband's suggestion, she took up psychometry, and was able to receive vivid impressions of events or people connected with an object just by holding it in her hand for a short time.

A pharaoh's life

In 1936 the psychic was given a scarab and whenever she handled it she recalled events of what appeared to be a previous life in Egypt. In 200 sessions she dictated the story of her existence as Sekeeta, the daughter of a pharaoh and later a priest-pharaoh herself. It amounted to 120,000 words and was published as Sekeeta's 'posthumous autobiography' under the title of *Winged pharaoh*.

What makes Sekeeta's story particularly fascinating is its claim that far memory was known and developed in Egyptian times. Those who received training in it had to remember at least 10 of their own deaths, and their graduation examination required them to be shut in a tomb for four days and nights, during which they underwent seven ordeals.

Sekeeta passed the test and seems to have brought her ability into the 20th century, remembering along the way lives in Greece in the second century BC, in medieval England and 16th-century Italy, and various others in Egypt.

Has Joan Grant really lived all these lives? Do we all have such a continuous past, spanning many centuries and civilisations? Her series of far-memory books and three autobiographical volumes insist that there is much more to life than the existence we are currently experiencing.

What is equally interesting is Joan Grant's claim that our present ills and problems may well have their roots in previous incarnations – and can be cured by far-memory recall of them.

within 24 hours of meeting, Joan and Esmond decided to become engaged.

Esmond had to go to France for six months on business and they planned to marry on his return. He spent the last few days before going abroad at the Marshall home. On the last night, as Esmond was walking to his bedroom, Joan heard a voice – she believes it was her grandmother's – say softly but distinctly: 'After Esmond leaves here tomorrow you will never see him again.'

On the night before he was due to return to England, Esmond died in an accident at a Paris shooting gallery with a gun he thought was not loaded.

Another dream in which a woman told her to 'Go to Leslie' sent Joan to Leslie Grant, whom she married in 1927 at the age of 20. Now she had an ally and a helper in her husband, who willingly undertook the job of writing down her dream experiences from

An aerial view of the burning of the French ship *Atlantique* off Guernsey on 4 January 1933. Joan Grant had a precognitive dream about the disaster. In it she was a French sailor caught in a ship fire. She even named the ship as the *Atlantic* and knew it was sailing the Channel

Have we shared previous lives with those who are close to us in this life? Can learning about traumas experienced in other lives relieve emotional problems?

JOAN GRANT HAS SUFFERED some dreadful deaths. She has been burned as a witch, been killed by a spear through the eye during a joust, and has bled to death when she ordered her Roman court physician to cut her wrists.

Twice she has committed suicide and twice she has died after being bitten by snakes. During a lifetime in Egypt, when she was a man, she was bitten by an insect and died from the infection. Another life ended when she broke her neck in a diving accident.

Joan Grant believes that everyone has had similar past lives, with deaths that are just as traumatic and horrifying. The difference is that most people can no longer remember their previous incarnations, whereas she has had a 'far memory' since childhood. Moreover, she has developed it to the extent that she can recall her earlier lives in exact detail.

Joan Grant perfected the technique of 'shifting the level of consciousness' between sleeping and waking so that she could dictate her dream experiences of previous lives. Seven books of these experiences have been published as historical novels, though she calls them 'posthumous autobiographies'. In addition, she has written about her experiences and abilities in this lifetime (*Far memory*, 1956) and her therapy work with her third husband, Dr Denys Kelsey (*Many lifetimes*, 1969).

The book for which she is best-known is

Breaking with the past

Above: Ramesses II, pharaoh of Egypt over 3000 years ago. Joan Grant believes that she lived as a man during his reign, a life she described in her book *So Moses was born*

Left: vultures savaging the carcase of a dead elephant. Vultures hovering over Alec Kerr-Clarkson in a previous incarnation created a phobia about touching bird feathers in this life. He overcame this fear when Joan Grant showed him the root cause of it by 'resonating' with his earlier self and discovering what had happened

Winged pharaoh (1937). It is the story of Sekeeta, a pharaoh's daughter, who became co-ruler with her brother when her father died. Sekeeta spent 10 years in a temple learning to recall her previous lives, an ability she has brought with her into the 20th century as Joan Grant. Sekeeta eventually qualified to be both a ruler and a priest: a winged pharaoh.

In another Egyptian life nearly 1000 years later, Joan Grant was a man: Ra-ab Hotep. His life appeared in two books, *Eyes of Horus* and *Lord of the horizon*, which were published in the early 1940s. *So Moses was born* (1952) dealt with a life when Joan Grant was a male contemporary of Ramesses II.

Joan Grant was born in England in 1907. As well as several lives in Egypt, she had incarnations in other places. In the 16th century she was in Italy, having been born Carola di Ludovici on 4 May 1510. She became a singer with a troupe of strolling players and died at the age of 27. In more recent times, she was an English girl named

Lavinia who broke her back in a fall from a horse. Lavinia died in 1875.

Taken at face value, it would seem that Joan Grant has lived numerous times before her present existence. But that, she says, is too simple an interpretation. She believes that our spirits are far greater than we realise and that each of the many other personalities she can recall has a soul. At death they become part of the whole spirit again. If, for some reason, the soul fails to integrate with the spirit, it produces a ghost. Joan Grant explains: 'Joan and Sekeeta are two beads on the same necklace and the memory they share is contained in the string.'

There are still wider implications to Joan Grant's far memory. She believes that many of the people who are close to us in this life have shared our lives in previous times. Sometimes they were husbands, sometimes wives. They may have been brothers or

Below: a witch being burned at the stake in the late Middle Ages in Germany. In one of her previous lives, Joan Grant believes she died just such a horrible death

Bottom: a group of strolling players rehearsing in 18th-century England. Joan Grant recalls leading the life of a singer with a troupe like this – but in Italy 200 years previously

hypnosis, at which he became adept. In addition, 'a series of cases came my way which, step by step, extended the framework of what I believed to be fact until, after four years, a session with a particular patient forced me to the intellectual certainty that in a human being there is a component which is not physical.'

Joan Grant's first book had a profound effect on Dr Denys Kelsey. He records in *Many lifetimes*: 'Before I had finished *Winged pharaoh* . . . I knew beyond any possibility of doubt, that reincarnation was a reality. . . . I would have journeyed halfway round the world to meet the author, but fortunately such a long pilgrimage proved unnecessary.' He discovered they lived only 30 miles (50 kilometres) apart. They met in 1958, and within two months 'embarked upon life together'.

Dr Kelsey had anticipated that his knowledge of hypnosis would link with Joan Grant's knowledge of reincarnation. What he did not realise, until they met, was that Joan had already worked closely with a psychiatrist during the war years and had gained a good deal of psychiatric experience. Now, working as a team, they were able to offer help to many people with a unique form of psychotherapy having its roots in past lives.

Joan Grant knew from her own experience that events in her previous incarnations, such as violent deaths, could have an effect on her present existence. On one occasion, for example, she battled unsuccessfully with herself for one hour in an attempt to pick up a slow-worm. She knew she was in no danger. But part of her was still 'resonating' to a stored memory of agonising pain in three snake-bite episodes in previous lives, two of which proved fatal.

While working in the laboratory of her

sisters, sons or daughters, lovers or friends. Our spirit, she asserts, is androgynous and therefore we incarnate in both male and female form. This makes for a wide range of personal relationships over time.

For example, one of the greatest influences on Joan Grant's early life was Daisy Sartorius, a family friend. It was while holding a scarab belonging to Daisy Sartorius that Joan Grant began recalling her previous life as Sekeeta, in the First Dynasty of Egypt about 3000 BC. In that existence, Joan discovered, Daisy had been her mother.

Similar connections were found between previous lives and her third husband, Dr Denys Kelsey. It was Denys Kelsey, a physician and psychiatrist, who cut the veins in Joan's wrists in Roman times on her orders, when he was also a physician. They later shared a life together as husband and wife in 18th-century England.

Dr Kelsey worked in the psychiatric wing at a military hospital in 1948. In trying to help the patients, he discovered the value of

father's Mosquito Control Institute, she had often given blood meals to the mosquitoes as part of her job. She had never had any ill effects. However, on several subsequent occasions, when she had mosquito bites on her eyelid, they produced a totally disproportionate amount of swelling and suffering. The reason, she discovered, was a resonance with her previous existence as an Egyptian captain. A bite on his eyelid, though from a fly, had led to what was probably septicaemia – and death.

According to Joan Grant and Denys Kelsey, once the causes of fears and anxieties are known and understood by bringing them into normal waking consciousness, the latent energy contained in them is defused. The soul can then be properly integrated and the problem usually disappears.

With the discovery that she could resonate with other people's past lives, Joan Grant found she was able to rid individuals of their apparently irrational fears when such emotion was a throw-back to previous times.

An early case, which occurred during her second marriage, concerned a psychiatrist, Alec Kerr-Clarkson. He visited her to discuss the possibility of reincarnation research. At the end of a pleasant weekend, he was about to leave the house to catch a train back to the north of England when her then husband, Charles Beatty, offered him a brace of pheasants, tied by the neck with a loop of string. The psychiatrist, looking embarrassed, backed away and asked if they could be wrapped in a parcel. Charles insisted they would travel better unwrapped, at which point Alec Kerr-Clarkson admitted, 'But I can't touch feathers.' No sooner had he said that than Joan Grant added:

As a young woman, Joan Grant battled with herself to pick up a slow-worm, which repelled her. She later learned through her 'far memory' that this was a reaction against three very unpleasant experiences with snakes in her past lives – two of which ended in her death

The reason you can't touch feathers is because you had a death which was very similar to one of mine. You were left among the dead on a battlefield. . . . Vultures are watching you . . . six vultures. You are very badly wounded, but you can still move your arms. Every time you move, the vultures hop a little further away. But then they hop closer again. . . . Now they are so close that you can smell them . . . they are beginning to tear at your flesh.

This account caused the psychiatrist to collapse on a sofa, sweating profusely, and he needed little persuasion to stay another night. Joan Grant spent most of the night at his bedside, during which time she realised what his problem was. He had begun to recall the episode himself quite vividly. 'Why did they leave me to die alone . . . why?' he cried out. 'Every other man had a friend to cut his throat . . . why did they betray me. . . . Me!'

It was this feeling of betrayal associated with the vultures that had created the feather phobia. Once Joan Grant was able to convince him that his comrades had not deliberately left him to a slow and painful death, having thought he was already dead, he was cured.

Using hypnosis, Dr Kelsey was able to produce similar past-life recalls in troubled patients. Joan Grant helped the therapy by resonating with the patient's experience and giving more details. Sometimes it was not even necessary for the patient to relive the experience. This happened in the case of a youth who had a severe anxiety problem. One day his parents telephoned to say he had tried to commit suicide that day. Joan Grant decided to delve into his past lives on her own

Above: Hurtwood, in Surrey, home of Daisy Sartorius. Joan Grant lived here for a number of years following a personal tragedy. During that time, she recalled her life as Sekeeta – and found out that Daisy Sartorius had been her mother then

Below: Dr Denys Kelsey, husband of Joan Grant, in his army days. The two worked in a psychiatric practice together for many years, and Kelsey still has a practice in their home at Pangbourne in Berkshire

to find out what was troubling him.

Dr Kelsey later was startled to find his wife in a distressed state. She was obviously in acute pain and tears were rolling down her face. He soon realised that she was reliving an episode in a previous life of the young patient. She told him:

> I can feel the blood clots in the tooth sockets. . . . It was bad enough during the first two days, after he pulled out all her teeth, but then the taste got worse and worse, not only dead blood but pus. Then the fever started . . . and she died on the fourth day.

It turned out that the woman concerned had had beautiful teeth that had been pulled out with nail pincers by a jealous husband. The youth had been that woman in a previous life and also had beautiful teeth in his present incarnation.

Dr Kelsey remembered that, in an early session, the troubled youth had said the anxiety problem had begun after an incident in a bar when another youth had threatened: 'I'm going to kick your teeth in!'

When told of Joan Grant's experience and the belief that he had had all his teeth wrenched out by a husband in the 19th century, the young man had no difficulty in accepting it. His anxiety disappeared instantly. Five years later, when Dr Kelsey and Joan Grant wrote about the case, it had not recurred.

Only a small number of people can be helped in this way, but Joan Grant believes that the message contained in her books will help many more. It is, very simply, to view this life – whatever its difficulties and sorrows – as just one of numerous others that will present us with challenges and opportunities to improve ourselves and help others.

The world of Uri Geller

Uri Geller's metal-bending magic has made him famous throughout the world. But how does he perform such baffling feats? What is the source of his remarkable power? COLIN WILSON investigates

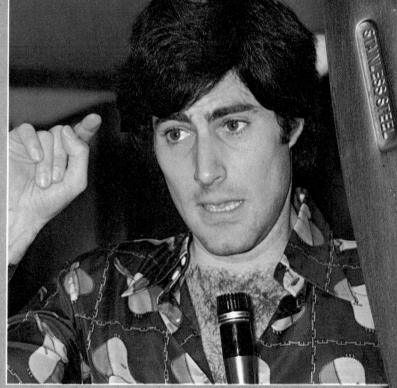

IN THE SUMMER of 1971, the teenagers of Israel were beginning to talk about a new pop idol – not a singer or a disc jockey, but a stage magician. His name was Uri Geller, and his popularity was undoubtedly influenced by the fact that he was tall, good-looking, and only 24 years old. But the act itself was startlingly original. Who had ever heard of a 'magician' repairing broken watches by merely looking at them? Or bending spoons by gently massaging them with his finger? Or breaking metal rings without even touching them? Yet these were just a few of the 'tricks' in Geller's dazzling repertoire.

Tales of this 'magic' reached the ears of a well-known psychical researcher named Andrija Puharich, who was so intrigued that he flew from New York to Israel to investigate. On 17 August 1971, Uri Geller was performing at a discotheque in Jaffa, and it was there that Puharich went to see him.

The first thing that struck him was that Geller was a born showman; he obviously loved performing in front of an audience. Yet Puharich found most of his act disappointing. Geller began with a demonstration of mindreading. He was blindfolded, then members of the audience were asked to write words on a blackboard. It was impossible for Geller to see the board; yet he guessed correctly every time. The enthusiasm of the teenage audience showed that they found it amazing; but Puharich knew that such feats are simple if the magician has a few confederates in the audience.

But the last 'trick' impressed him more. Geller announced that he would break a ring without touching it, and a woman in the audience offered her dress ring. She was told

to show it to the audience, then hold it tightly in her hand. Geller placed his own hand above hers and held it there for a few seconds. When she opened her hand, the ring had snapped in two.

After the show, Puharich asked Geller if he would submit to a few scientific tests the next day. So far, Geller had consistently refused to be examined by 'experts'. But this time he readily agreed – to his own surprise, as he later admitted. It was a fateful decision: Geller's first step on the road to world fame.

Geller duly arrived at Puharich's apartment the next day. And his first demonstration convinced Puharich that this was genuine 'magic'. Geller placed a notepad on the table, then asked Puharich to think of three numbers. Puharich chose 4, 3 and 2:

Geller began giving demonstrations of his powers in 1968, first to groups of school children and at private parties, then to large audiences in theatres all over Israel. He said he was surprised at how well the experiments worked in front of so many people – having an audience even seemed to help

'Now turn that notepad over,' said Geller. Puharich did, and found himself looking at the figures 4, 3 and 2 – written *before* he had thought of the numbers. Geller had somehow 'influenced' him into choosing those three figures.

The point is worth remembering, for it suggests that Geller could hypnotise people by means of 'telepathy'. Yet whether this helps to explain the weird and incredible events that followed is open to debate.

At further demonstrations, Geller went on to raise the temperature of a thermometer by staring at it, move a compass needle by concentrating on it, and bend a stream of water from a tap by moving his finger close to it. Puharich's conclusion was that Uri Geller was no mere conjuror: he was a genuine psychic, with a definite power of 'mind over matter' – a faculty known as psychokinesis.

Geller admitted that he had no idea of how he came to possess these curious powers. He had become aware of them when he was little more than a baby. At the age of six, he realised he could read his mother's mind. She came back one day from a party at which she had played cards for money. Geller took one look at her, and was able to tell her precisely how much she had lost.

When he started to go to school, his stepfather gave him a watch. But it always seemed to be going wrong. One day, as Geller stared at it, the hands began to go faster and faster, until they were whirling around. It was then that he began to suspect he might be causing it. Yet he seemed to have no control over this freakish ability. One day, when he was eating soup in a restaurant, the bowl fell off the spoon. Then spoons and forks on nearby tables began to bend. Geller's parents were so worried they even thought of taking him to see a psychiatrist.

By the age of 13, he was beginning to gain some kind of control over his powers. He broke a lock on a bicycle by concentrating on it, and learned to cheat at exams by reading the minds of more diligent pupils – he said he

American psychical researcher Andrija Puharich who investigated Uri Geller in the early 1970s. His account of his experiences with Geller was published in 1974 and made the astonishing claim that Geller was the messenger of the Nine, a group of extra-terrestrial beings who were the 'controllers of the Universe'

only had to stare at the backs of their heads to see the answers.

Puharich was intensely excited; it looked as if he had made the find of the century. Ever since the formation of the Society for Psychical Research in 1882, scientists have been studying psychics and mediums, trying to prove or disprove their claims. They have never succeeded in doing either. And the reason is mainly that most psychics claim they cannot switch their powers on and off at will. Yet Geller's powers seemed to work to order, whenever he wanted them to. If they would work in a laboratory as well as on stage, it would be one of the greatest triumphs in the history of psychical research.

At this point, events took a completely unexpected turn. On the morning of 1 December 1971 Geller was hypnotised by Puharich in the hope of uncovering clues about the origin of his powers. Puharich asked him where he was; Geller replied that he was in a cave in Cyprus – where his family had lived

Interest in Geller and his paranormal powers grew rapidly and a multitude of books about him appeared in the 1970s. Geller himself is an author – his autobiography, *My story*, was published in 1975, and many of his poems, which he says seem to 'come through' him rather than being composed by him, have been set to music and recorded

when he was 13 – and that he was 'learning about people who come from space.' He added that he was not yet allowed to talk about this. Puharich regressed him further, and Geller began to speak in Hebrew – the first language he had learned. At this point he described an episode that, he said, had taken place when he was three years old. He had walked into a garden in Tel Aviv, and suddenly become aware of a shining, bowl-like object floating in the air above his head. There was a high, ringing sound in the air. As the object came closer, Uri felt himself bathed in light, and fell down in a faint.

As Geller recounted these events, Puharich and his fellow investigators were startled to hear a voice speaking from the air above their heads. Puharich described it as 'unearthly and metallic'. 'It was we who found Uri in the garden when he was three,' said the disembodied voice. 'He is our help-er, sent to help man. We programmed him in the garden.' The reason, it explained, was that mankind was on the point of a world war. Uri, it implied, had been 'programmed' to avert the catastrophe.

The voice stopped speaking. When Geller woke up, he seemed to have no memory of what had happened; so Puharich played the tape back. As he listened to his voice recounting the episode in the garden, Geller looked worried. 'I can't remember any of this.' And then, as the metallic voice began to speak, Geller snatched the cassette off the recorder. As he held it in his hand, it vanished. Then Geller rushed from the room. When they found him, some time later, he seemed to be

Geller's powers began to manifest themselves when he was a small child: he found that he could read his mother's mind, affect the workings of clocks and watches simply by looking at them, and cause spoons and forks to bend or break. At first his parents were merely embarrassed by the extraordinary events that occurred, but then they became concerned that something was wrong with him, and even considered consulting a psychiatrist

confused, and there was no sign of the tape.

What had happened? The sceptical explanation is that Geller performed a little ven-triloquism, then palmed the tape and made sure it 'disappeared', so that subsequent tests would not reveal the resemblance between his own voice and the 'space being' on the tape. But Puharich and the others said the voice came from above their heads, and that it sounded mechanical, as if manufactured by a computer. And even if Geller could have tricked a number of trained observers on this first occasion, it would certainly have been quite impossible on some later occasions described by Puharich. For the bodiless voice was only the first in a series of weird and inexplicable events – events that finally destroyed all Puharich's hopes of convincing the world that Geller's powers were genuine.

These events are described by Puharich in his book *Uri: a journal of the mystery of Uri Geller*. And they sound so confused and preposterous that the reader ends by doubt-ing Puharich's common sense, then his san-ity. He describes how, the following day, he recorded yet another hypnotic session with Geller, and how the 'voice' again interrupted and talked about war. Then Puharich and Geller went for a drive, taking the recorder with them, and the tape suddenly vanished into thin air. From then on, hardly a day went past without the mysterious 'entities' performing some mind-boggling trick to convince Puharich of their reality. They made the car engine stop, and then start up again. They 'teleported' Puharich's briefcase from his house in New York to his apartment in Tel Aviv. When Geller and Puharich went to an army base to entertain the troops, they were followed by a red light in the sky that was invisible to their military escort. Geller actually photographed a 'space ship' on the orders of the metallic voice.

Was it a joke? Or some kind of trickery? Puharich, at least, was convinced that no

fraud was involved. A few years before, a psychic had given him messages from some mysterious beings who called themselves the 'Nine', and who said they came from outer space. And at one of the hypnotic sessions with Geller, Puharich asked whether the voice was one of the Nine, and it answered 'Yes'. He went on to ask if the Nine were behind the UFO sightings that had been taking place since Kenneth Arnold saw the first 'flying saucer' in 1947; again the answer was 'Yes'. The voice told Puharich that the Nine were beings from another dimension, and that they lived in a star ship called *Spectra*, which was '53,069 light ages away'. They had been watching Earth for thousands of years, and had landed in South America 3000 years ago. And they would soon prove their existence by landing on planet Earth. . . .

It is easy to jeer at all this, and to condemn

Puharich for his gullibility. The simple explanation seems to be that Geller had been reading Erich von Däniken's *Chariots of the gods?* and decided to fool the naïve Puharich with this preposterous gobbledegook about space beings and star ships. Yet if Puharich's description of the various events is accurate, this is totally impossible. No doubt Geller could have palmed the cassettes, imitated the metallic voice, and faked the photograph of a UFO. But it is hard to see how he could have transported Puharich's briefcase from New York, caused the car engine to stop and start, and arranged for them to be followed by a red light that was invisible to the soldiers who were escorting them.

Could Puharich himself be telling lies? This hypothesis must also be ruled out. Puharich's aim was simply to prove that Geller possessed paranormal powers, and all he had to do was to arrange for scientific tests

A photograph taken on 4 November 1972 by Geller when travelling by jet from London to Munich. According to Geller, his camera rose into the air of its own accord and stopped in front of him, as if signalling him to take a picture. Geller could see nothing in the sky but nevertheless took several shots. When the film was developed, five frames contained images of UFOS alongside the aeroplane

of these powers – as he later did in the United States. Far from making his case more convincing or interesting, all this talk about *Spectra* and the Nine only makes it sound absurd. By writing about it, he only destroyed his own credibility.

Does this mean, then, that the Nine were genuine, and that they have really chosen Geller to be their emissary on Earth? This is equally difficult to accept – and Geller says that he himself does not accept it. Then what *does* he believe? The answer is: nothing. He declares that the events described by Puharich leave him totally bewildered, and that he has no idea of their explanation.

Geller himself was becoming rather worried by all these strange events by the beginning of 1972. Unlike Puharich, he had no desire to convince the scientific establishment of the reality of his powers; he was more interested in becoming rich and famous. And the bewildering tricks performed by the Nine seemed unlikely to bring him closer to that goal. The same thing applied to Puharich, with all his talk about scientific proof and laboratory testing. Geller must have heaved a sigh of relief when, in April 1972, Puharich flew back to New York, promising to return in a few weeks. He proceeded to finalise plans to display his psychic talents in Germany, under the guidance of a professional impressario.

A sign from the Nine

Another curious event, described in *Uri*, guaranteed that Geller was able to make this trip to Germany alone. According to Puharich, Geller went into his apartment on 1 June 1972, and found a letter from Puharich on the mat. It stated simply that Puharich was unable to leave the United States for another three months, and would join Geller later. Accordingly, Geller flew on to Rome – en route for Munich – and telephoned Puharich to ask about the delay. Puharich was amazed, and denied writing any such letter. At which point, it struck them both that the letter must be yet another 'sign' from the Nine. The 'proof' was that it had vanished from Geller's shirt-pocket while he was on the aeroplane – obviously dematerialised by the owner of the metallic voice. A simpler explanation might be that Geller had invented the letter. But then, its appearance and disappearance are no more incredible than all the other baffling events described by Puharich.

Whatever the explanation, the letter incident convinced Puharich that the Nine wanted him to remain behind in the United States, trying to convince various eminent scientists that Geller was worth investigating. Meanwhile, his volatile and unpredictable protégé flew on to Munich, to keep his first appointment with fame and fortune – or at least, with notoriety and publicity.

Under the eyes of scientists

After a successful tour of Germany it seemed that Uri Geller had at last been accepted as a genuine psychic. But in the USA he was not so well received

URI GELLER ARRIVED in Munich in June 1972, and immediately displayed that gift for publicity that would make him the most famous – and the richest – 'psychic' in the world. The tour had been arranged by an agent named Yasha Katz, who made sure that Geller was met by crowds of reporters. One of them asked him: 'What can you do that would be really astounding?' 'Suggest something,' said Geller. 'How about stopping a cable car in mid-air? After a moment's hesitation, Geller said: 'Sure, why not.' And the crowd of goggle-eyed reporters trailed behind him to the Hochfelln funicular line outside Munich.

The car left on its journey to the mountain top, and Geller concentrated hard. Nothing happened. It came down again, and still nothing happened. Then up and down again. By this time, Geller's confidence had drained away, and the reporters were losing interest. Then suddenly, to everyone's astonishment,

the cable car stopped in mid-air. The mechanic called the control centre – and was told that the main switch had suddenly flipped off. Minutes later, the reporters were scrambling to get to the nearest telephones.

Inevitably, they wanted him to do something else. Someone suggested stopping an escalator in a department store. This time, Geller's luck seemed to have run out. Up and down, up and down they went. Then, at the twentieth attempt, the escalator stopped. . . .

Not surprisingly there were sceptics who felt that the amazing feat could be explained by a large bribe to a friendly electrician. Yet Geller also impressed a German scientist, Friedbert Karger, with his ring-breaking trick. Karger held the ring tightly in his hand; Geller held his own hand above it for a few moments – and when Karger opened his hand, the ring was broken. Karger was so excited that he rang Geller's mentor, Andrija Puharich, in New York, suggesting that Geller should stay on in Germany to be thoroughly investigated by scientists. Puharich squashed that one. Geller was already booked by some of America's most eminent scientific investigators.

Geller himself was not that enthusiastic

Geller and the cable car that halted halfway up the mountainside after he had been concentrating on stopping it. This was just one of the 'stunts' Geller performed in Germany in 1972

either. He was tasting fame, and enjoying the flavour. One impressario even wanted Geller to play in a musical about 'unknown powers', and Geller loved the idea. When told about all this over the telephone, Puharich gave a heartfelt sigh, and flew to Germany. And the young celebrity was persuaded to drop his plans to become the world's first singing mystic, and accompany his distraught Svengali back to the United States.

In fact, he was not too difficult to persuade. After weeks of non-stop exposure in the German media, Geller's feats were beginning to lose their impact on the public.

One of the oddest things about the Geller story is that he failed to achieve the same instant fame in the United States that he had found in Germany. There seem to be two explanations. One is that the Americans are hardened to publicity, and tend to become sceptical at the sight of 'miracle workers'. The other is that Geller's reputation had preceded him, and he found himself faced with considerable 'sales resistance'. Tales about Puharich's new protégé had already reached the world of paranormal research in the United States – a world in which Puharich was regarded as an eminent scientific investigator. According to the rumours, Puharich had been completely 'taken in' by this Israeli 'pop-magician', even to believing that he was an emissary from outer space. There were whispers that Geller was Puharich's 'evil genius'. So when Geller arrived in New York in the autumn of 1972, he found the atmosphere distinctly chilly.

From the beginning, he was surrounded by eminent scientists – men like Ed Mitchell, the Moon astronaut, Wernher von Braun, inventor of the v-2 rocket, and the physicist Gerald Feinberg. Geller was suspicious and unhappy; yet his powers seemed to be working excellently. In von Braun's office, he performed an interesting variant on his ring-breaking, flattening the gold wedding ring

In the years since he began demonstrating his powers, Uri Geller has been seen to bend thousands of metal objects, either by stroking the metal lightly with his finger or simply by concentrating on it. In some cases the object has continued to bend after it has left his hand

Geller with John Lennon, talking about UFOs. Geller became interested in UFOS when he heard the voice of a 'space being' talking about the starship *Spectra*. After that, he claimed to have seen a 'red, disc-shaped light' that seemed to be following him, and managed to capture UFOS on film – even though he had not seen them in the sky at the time he took the photographs

that von Braun held tightly in his own hand. Then von Braun found that his calculator battery was flat, although it had been put in that morning. Geller held the calculator between his hands. And when von Braun pushed the 'on' switch, the battery was no longer dead, but the display flashed random numbers. Geller had another try, and this time the calculator worked normally. There was no way in which it could have been faked – even a conjuror cannot get at the circuitry of a sealed calculator. Von Braun concluded that Geller could produce some strange electrical currents – a reasonable and probably correct assumption.

Return of the 'space spooks'

In spite of these successes, Geller was tense and miserable. Apart from anything else, the 'space spooks' were at it again. In a room in a Washington hotel, an ashtray floated off the table, as if moved by invisible hands. Then the tape recorder began to work of its own accord. When Puharich – who was present – played the tape back, the weird metallic voice they had first heard in 1971 spoke again, explaining that the starship *Spectra* would soon be making a landing on Earth – but only for refuelling. The 'mass landing' promised in earlier interviews was evidently to come later. They also – to Puharich's surprise and irritation – told him not to start experiments with Geller for the time being, and not to tell anyone about these strange messages. When all this was over, the tape – according to Puharich – simply dissolved into thin air. Later messages that arrived through the tape recorder again insisted that Puharich should

'storm', his friendly black labrador dog suddenly bit Geller on the wrist. The day before this same dog had suddenly vanished from the kitchen before their eyes, and a few moments later, was seen walking towards the house from 70 yards (65 metres) away – mysteriously 'teleported' by the space men, according to Puharich, to demonstrate their power. But perhaps the dog knew better. Perhaps it knew intuitively that the real culprit was Geller himself – or rather a stranger living in Geller's unconscious mind.

A few days later, the scientific tests began. They were held at the Stanford Research Institute in California, and conducted by Dr Hal Puthoff and Russell Targ. And as soon as the tests began, Geller knew he had nothing to worry about. Most psychics find it hard to perform under laboratory conditions; Geller

scrap his plans for scientific tests. Understandably, Puharich was distraught. These beings from outer space – if that is where they came from – were wrecking his plans. Even Geller was unexpectedly sceptical; in one indignant outburst he said that he thought the 'space beings' were clowns playing practical jokes.

All this culminated in one highly significant event that Puharich dismisses in a single paragraph in his book on Geller, yet that could well provide the key to the mystery.

A psychic storm

When Puharich told Geller that he intended to ignore the 'space beings', and go ahead with the plans for scientific testing, Geller lost his temper and hurled a sugar bowl at his head. Puharich exploded in violent indignation. At that moment, an immense wind blew up outside, shaking the trees, and a grandfather clock shot across the hall and shattered into a thousand pieces. Overawed but still determined, Geller begged Puharich to forget the scientists. Puharich dug in his heels, and eventually won his point.

These incredible events – assuming that Puharich is reporting them accurately – may seem to confirm that some 'superhuman' powers were involved. Yet every paranormal researcher is aware that poltergeists can often produce equally amazing effects. And there is general agreement that poltergeists are closely connected with the unconscious minds of some human being or beings.

If the 'space beings' really existed, why should they suddenly order Puharich to drop the scientific investigations that they had earlier approved? On the other hand, if the strange manifestations originated in Uri Geller's unconscious mind, it would be perfectly understandable. He wanted to be famous and (if possible) rich, and the idea of being tested by sceptical scientists worried him. Significantly, the one project to which the 'space beings' gave the go-ahead was a film about the life of Geller.

Puharich tells how, the morning after the

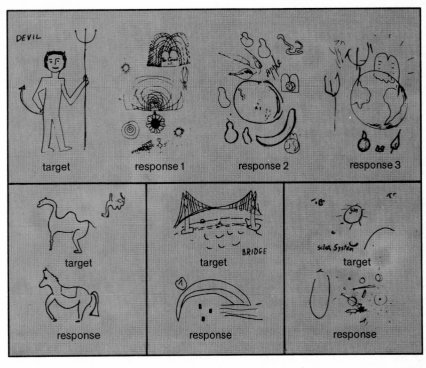

Target pictures and responses drawn by Geller during the SRI series of tests. Before each experiment Geller was isolated from the researchers in a shielded room – only then was the target chosen and a picture drawn

had no such problems. As soon as he began to concentrate on trying to bend a brass ring out of shape, the television monitor through which he was being watched began to distort, and its distortions occurred every time Geller's face distorted with concentration. Obviously, he was producing some kind of mysterious electrical effect. At the same moment, a computer on the floor below began to go wrong.

Next, Geller was tested for extra-sensory perception (ESP). Here his success was spectacular. A die was placed in a closed box and shaken; then Geller was asked to guess which side was uppermost. His guesses were right every time. Ten empty cans were placed upside down on a table, with a small object hidden under one of them; then Geller was brought into the room and asked to guess which can concealed the object. Again, his score was incredible – 12 out of 14 correct guesses. He was then asked to try to duplicate drawings sealed inside double envelopes; again and again, his response was breathtakingly accurate. Yet when 'target drawings' were selected at random from a huge pile made by many people in the building – so that the experimenters themselves had no idea of what was in the sealed envelope – Geller's score fell dramatically. This suggests that his success in the drawing experiments depends heavily upon telepathy or 'mindreading'. Yet this failed to explain the experiments with the dice, which prove genuine ESP *without* telepathy.

Challenged by the sceptics

Just as it seemed that Geller had passed his most difficult tests, and proved the genuineness of his powers, his American visit began to go badly wrong. He was asked to present himself at the offices of *Time* magazine; but the 'photographer' who made the appointment was, in fact, a professional 'magician' named Charles Reynolds. Puharich guessed that the magicians of America were plotting to 'lynch' Geller – and he was right. James Randi – one of the most celebrated illusionists since Houdini – was convinced that Geller was a fake, and was determined to expose him. Puharich was inclined to refuse to allow Geller to be tried by this kangaroo court of stage magicians; but Geller realised that his refusal would only be interpreted as guilt. So on 6 February 1973, he and Puharich presented themselves at the *Time* offices.

Geller was understandably nervous, faced with the obvious hostility of two 'magicians' and two *Time* editors. But he succeeded in demonstrating his telepathic powers by duplicating a drawing in a sealed envelope. After this, he bent a fork by stroking it lightly with his finger; the fork went on bending after he put it down. Charles Reynolds offered Geller his own apartment key – to make sure there could be no 'switching' – and Geller bent it by concentrating; again, the key continued to

Above: Russell Targ who, with Harold Puthoff, conducted the experiments on Geller at Stanford in 1972

Right: stage magician James Randi is convinced that Uri Geller is a fraud, and claims that he can duplicate every one of Geller's 'paranormal' effects. Here Randi demonstrates his own apparent control over metal: he was handcuffed and locked into a high security bank safe – and escaped in less than four minutes

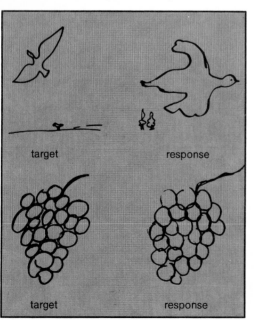

More target pictures and Geller's responses during the SRI tests. Geller's success with the 'grape' target is astonishing: he drew exactly the same number of circles as in the original drawing

bend after it had left his hand. On the whole, Geller performed very creditably, and might have been justified in expecting a favourable report. In fact, the article that appeared in *Time* a few weeks later was damning. The two magicians claimed that they could easily duplicate every one of Geller's 'tricks', and that Randi actually did so after Geller had left the office. It ended by stating – quite untruthfully – that Geller had been forced to leave Israel in disgrace after a computer expert and some psychologists had duplicated his feats and accused him of fraud.

Randi and Charles Reynolds even asserted later that they themselves had caught Geller cheating – or at least, had seen him bending the fork by pressing it against the desk. Oddly enough, this extremely important accusation is not mentioned in the *Time*

article – which seems strange in view of its determination to prove Geller a fake.

As far as the great American public was concerned, the Geller myth had now been exploded; he had been 'proved' to be a mere trickster. And since *Time* had such an immense worldwide circulation, there was little that either Geller or Puharich could do about it. By the end of March 1973, it looked as if the amazing career of Uri Geller had come to an end – a mere 18 months or so after it had begun. Yet as Puharich sat down at his desk, and wrote the opening lines of his book *Uri: a journal of the mystery of Uri Geller*, he experienced a quiet conviction that there was more to come.

What Geller experienced was more than quiet conviction; it was an outraged determination to make the sceptics eat their words.

The psychic superstar

Scientific investigation largely redeemed Uri Geller from accusations of fraud, but the controversy still raged.

FAME ARRIVED FOR URI GELLER on the evening of 23 November 1973 when he appeared on BBC-TV's *David Dimbleby Talk-in*. Overnight, that television programme turned Geller into the most controversial man in the British Isles.

By his own standards, the feats Geller performed that evening were not spectacular. With his eyes closed, he duplicated a drawing that had been made just before the programme and sealed in an envelope. Then he bent a fork – which Dimbleby held in his own hand – by gently stroking it. He started two broken watches by rubbing them, and caused the hands of one of them to bend upwards inside the glass. A fork on the table began to bend of its own accord. At the end of the programme, the producer came on to announce that they had received dozens of telephone calls from viewers saying that their own forks and spoons had begun to bend.

The next morning, there was probably not a single office or factory in England where Geller was not the main topic of conversation. Possibly the British are more gullible than the Americans. Or possibly, as J. B. Priestley once suggested, they are simply less accustomed to high-pressure advertising, and therefore less cynical. Not that there was any absence of cynicism after the programme. One journalist stated authoritatively

Uri Geller at the first World Congress of Sorcery in Bogotá, Colombia, in 1975. Geller was billed as the main attraction of the show, the intention of which was 'to discuss and analyse the New Dimensions of Man and Life'. Besides demonstrating his power to bend metal, Geller started 50 broken watches, including one that, its owner claimed, had not worked for 40 years

that Geller had invented a powder that could cause metal to crumble instantaneously – then had to admit this was pure speculation. The science editor of the *Sunday Times*, Brian Silcock, was also a sceptic, until he rode with Geller in a taxi to the airport, and offered his own front door key for experiment. The moment Geller began to stroke it with one finger, the key bent like melting wax.

Metal bending nationwide

The excitement in England was reported all round the world. After two false starts – in Germany and the United States – Geller had achieved what he always wanted: the instantaneous fame of a pop star. Even the Americans, who had declined to take him seriously, suddenly had second thoughts: when Geller went back there later, they made up for their former indifference and treated him like a returning hero. Meanwhile, in England, a Sunday newspaper – the *People* – organised an experiment at short notice. They announced that at noon on the Sunday following the broadcast, Geller would concentrate his powers, and try to make spoons and forks bend all over England. They asked readers to report any such phenomena. The following Sunday, they described the flood of mail and telephone calls that began soon after the appointed time; 300 spoons and forks had curled up, and over 1000 broken clocks and watches had started up again.

The British seem to have broken the 'scepticism barrier'. Only two days after his triumph on the Dimbleby programme, Geller was demonstrating his powers in

Paris; then he moved on to Scandinavia, Spain, Italy and Japan. Luck – or perhaps his guardians from outer space – continued to favour him with amazing coincidences. In Oslo, he told a reporter jokingly that his psychic powers could fuse lights – and all the street lights in Oslo fused. On a ship in the Mediterranean, Geller said he would try stopping the ship – and a few minutes later, it slowed down and stopped. (A crimped fuel line was found to be the cause.)

Back in the United States, he received the kind of attention and adulation he had hoped for the first time – and also discovered that old enemies like Charles Reynolds and James Randi had lost none of their hostility. *Time* magazine once again denounced him, and took the opportunity to pour scorn on the whole 'psychic' scene, from Kirlian photography and psychic surgery to the 'secret life of plants'. Reynolds and Randi took this belated opportunity to assert that they had seen Geller bending a fork manually against the desk in the previous *Time* interview, although they failed to explain why they had withheld this important piece of information for so long. On the other hand, the publication of the report from the Stanford Research Institute – in the influential magazine *Nature* – convinced many scientists that

Right: housewife Dora Portman of Harrow, England, was listening to a radio programme featuring Uri Geller in November 1973. Geller invited listeners to hold a piece of cutlery and try to bend it by concentration. To Mrs Portman's surprise the ladle she was using suddenly began to bend and the enamel to crack

Geller's powers were basically genuine. And the affirmative reports of various British scientists – like John Taylor and Ted Bastin – supported this view. (John Taylor, however, has since concluded that there is nothing paranormal about Geller's powers.) So instead of being merely the helpless victim of a campaign of defamation, Geller was now a figure of controversy.

Now that all the controversy has died down, and Uri Geller is merely another one of those names of the 1970s, a nine days' wonder that no longer causes wonderment, we can look back on his remarkable career,

Geller with David Dimbleby, experimenting with a key. Geller's appearance on BBC-TV's *David Dimbleby Talk-in* programme on 23 November 1973 was an outstanding success, and convinced scientists that he was worthy of serious scientific investigation

and see that Puharich was right from the beginning. What Geller really needed was to be studied by scientists, not exposed in front of television cameras. A film star or a pop singer has a firm foundation for celebrity; people all over the world are still listening to the records of Bob Dylan and Elvis Presley, or watching old movies of James Dean and Marilyn Monroe. But once you had seen Geller bend a spoon on television, there was nothing more to look forward to – except watching him bend a fork on some other programme. Geller himself was painfully aware of this: he wrote an autobiography; he wrote a novel; he made persistent attempts to star in a film about his own life. And he submitted to hundreds of scientific tests.

The essence of all this investigation is published in a remarkable volume called *The Geller papers*. It makes impressive reading, and demonstrates beyond all doubt that Geller possesses some kind of paranormal powers. Yet because he achieved his main celebrity as a 'magician' on television, Geller has suffered the fate of so many overnight celebrities, and become merely a half-remembered name.

A personal view

My own acquaintance with Geller began when he was at the height of his fame, in 1974. My agent rang me one day and asked me if I would be interested in writing a biography of Uri Geller. I said no. I had just read Puharich's book, which had been one of the major publishing disasters of the year. All his incredible stories about disembodied

not too impressed. I knew enough about conjuring to know that the spoon bending and watch-changing could have been sleight of hand, and the fact that he had to cross the restaurant to bend a key struck me as suspicious. Yet he performed one feat that left me in no doubt of his genuineness.

What happened was this: Geller turned his back on me, so he looked out over the restaurant (I was in a corner), and asked me to do a drawing on the back of the menu card. I did a sketch of a funny monster I draw for my children. I kept glancing at Geller to make sure he wasn't peeping, or holding a mirror in his hand. Then he made me turn the menu over and cover it with my hand. He turned round again, and asked me to redraw the thing *in my mind*, and try to convey it to him. After a couple of false starts, he suddenly drew a duplicate of the 'monster' on the menu. There was no way in which he could have 'guessed' it, or that Rae Knight might have conveyed it to him – even if she had been an accomplice.

An odd coincidence

A few months later, when asked to write a short book about Geller, I travelled to Barcelona to see him – it struck me only later that his first question to me had been: 'Are you anything to do with Spain?' – an odd coincidence. Again objects fell from the air, and Geller demonstrated metal bending and mindreading. In the office of my Spanish publisher he silenced the sceptical audience by holding up a spoon by its end, and bending it by simply 'tickling' the thin part with his index finger – no kind of pressure would have been possible. He placed his foot against a radiator as he did this.

My own study of Geller has convinced me that his powers are genuine. His mindreading was particularly convincing. James Randi – who likes to call himself the 'Amazing Randi' – declared that he could easily

voices speaking out of tape recorders, and dogs being 'teleported' down the garden, sounded too absurd to be taken seriously. A 'straight' book about Geller's psychic abilities would probably have been a bestseller; but the miracle-working inhabitants of the starship *Spectra* turned the whole thing into farce.

Geller, it seemed, had persuaded the famous impressario Robert Stigwood – producer of *Hair* and *Jesus Christ superstar* (and later of *Saturday night fever*) – to back the idea of a film about his life. First of all, someone had to write the life. When I declined, they suggested that I might like to work on a film script. And as the pay – for an underpaid student of the paranormal – was generous, I decided it might be worth looking into.

I met Geller at Robert Stigwood's offices in London. He seemed a charming and unassuming young man, whose enthusiasm seems to keep his whole personality on rather a high note. As I walked into the office he asked me: 'Are you anything to do with Spain?' I looked blank. 'Just as you walked in that door, a coin jumped out of this tray on the desk – a Spanish peseta – it made me wonder if you had anything to do with Spain.' Stigwood's personal secretary, Rae Knight, verified that this had actually happened, and I later learned to regard her with total trust. They had both been on the opposite side of the room when the coin leapt across it.

At lunch in a nearby restaurant, Geller talked non-stop, made my watch go back several hours by simply holding his hand above it (he changed the date too), bent a spoon, and broke a key I had brought along by simply rubbing it. But he insisted on taking the key to the other side of the room, where there was a radiator – he said he could gain power from metal. On the whole, I was

Author Colin Wilson with Geller in Barcelona, discussing the nature of Geller's paranormal powers. Geller told him: 'I don't know where they come from or what they mean, or why it should be me and not somebody else'

Geller undergoing one of a series of tests designed to discover whether his physical make-up is responsible for the powers of his mind

duplicate any of Geller's 'tricks'; but when I met him, he was unable to duplicate the mindreading trick – although he offered to do it for me next day (obviously when he'd had time to prepare it). But Randi *did* bend spoons by stroking them and made my watch go back several hours by rubbing it.

The film on Geller never came off, although I made several 'outline' sketches. I continued to see and correspond with Geller, on and off, for a year or so, but lost touch with him when he moved to New York. In one of his later letters to me he mentioned that he had produced a tremendous impression in Mexico, and was a frequent guest at the home of the president. He also mentioned that he had taken up 'dowsing' for metals from an aeroplane, and made a considerable success of it, working for a mining company. From the financial point of view, I gather he has no reason to complain of the way the world has treated him. And if his spoon bending has ceased to attract much attention, this is hardly surprising. From Geller's point of view, I feel it is a pity it ever did.

And what do I feel about the source of his powers? After a great deal of thought, I am still inclined to believe that Geller is an unconscious 'medium', and that he simply produces more-or-less controlled 'poltergeist effects'. (That other remarkable psychic, Matthew Manning, whom I have also investigated, began his career as the unconscious 'focus' of a series of alarming poltergeist occurrences in his own home.) Geller told me how, at the age of three, he received a bad electric shock from his mother's sewing machine; this, I am inclined to believe, may have started the whole thing. It is surprising how often 'mediums' have had severe traumas or emotional strains in childhood.

'Unconscious mediums'

And what about the 'space men' from the starship *Spectra*? Here again, I believe that Geller's unconscious mind is the basic explanation. But I suspect there was more than that involved. In one of their mysterious 'interviews', the 'space men' told Puharich that he himself had psychic powers. I believe this to be almost certainly true. And the astounding series of events that began when Puharich and Geller got together in Tel Aviv were a kind of wild collaboration between two 'unconscious mediums'. Unlikely? I can only say that the more I have studied the evidence, the more I feel this is the case.

There is one more point. Spiritualists believe that there *are* such things as disembodied spirits, hanging around on the 'earth plane', and often getting into mischief. Such spirits may cause poltergeist effects. And the more I read the weird but inconsequential communications of the 'space beings' from *Spectra*, the more I am reminded of the confused and usually irrelevant material that emerges at so many seances.

These may not, I agree, be the correct explanations. But of one thing I am certain. There *is* something about Uri Geller that demands a deeper and more far-reaching explanation than mere trickery.

Professors John Hasted and John Taylor (above) carried out tests on Geller in 1974. Geller succeeded in bending metal strips sealed in plastic tubes (right). And he was asked to bend a brass strip taped to a letter balance so the pressure he applied could be measured. The scale read only half an ounce (15 grams), and the strip bent upwards, against the pressure of his fingers (far right)

A SMALL, CHUBBY FIGURE in a bright red robe and with a halo of crinkly black hair stood before a typically huge crowd eagerly awaiting him. He turned an empty hand palm down and began moving it in circles. When he turned it over it contained a gold necklace. The spectators were delighted. Satya Sai Baba had performed another miracle. The necklace is one of more than 10,000 objects he is said to have materialised in this way, including diamonds, gold rings, beads, books, religious idols and even food.

The miracles of Satya Sai Baba are so incredible that they invite disbelief. Yet the witnesses who have come forward to testify to his astonishing powers often have impeccable credentials: they include government officials, scientists and religious leaders.

His followers run into tens of thousands around the world, though the majority are in his native India which now has 3000 Sai centres to promote his teachings, and five Sai universities. Many of his devotees regard him as an *avatar* – a god incarnate. Colin Wilson describes him as a 'contemporary Hindu saint.' And others who have written about him find many parallels between his miracles and those of Christ.

When he was born on 23 November 1926, Satyanarayana Raju was a normal robust child, though he soon caused consternation by refusing to eat meat and bringing beggars

Man of many miracles

Above: Sai Baba as he is today. Significantly his robe has no pockets and only narrow wrists – there is nowhere he could hide the 'apports' he produces

Right: Sai Baba as a young man. The powers he possesses have always been special: his father even sought to have him exorcised

home so that his mother could feed them. At school he was fun-loving and popular. He would arrive early in order to conduct worship with other children, most of whom were attracted by his ability to dip his hand into an empty bag and bring out sweets, or everyday objects they had lost.

Despite these early signs that he was special, the Raju family had hopes that he would be well educated and become a government officer. Instead, a strange incident occurred when he was 13 which proved to be a turning point in his life.

While walking with friends he suddenly leapt in the air with a loud shriek, holding a toe of his right foot. Everyone thought he had been stung by a scorpion, but next day he showed no sign of pain or sickness . . . until the evening when he suddenly fell unconscious to the ground.

When he recovered consciousness next day he seemed to be another person: bursting

68

into song, reciting poetry and quoting long passages in Sanskrit that were far beyond his knowledge.

His worried parents consulted various doctors who prescribed different remedies, and when these failed to cure Satya they arranged for the 'demon' in him to be exorcised. The young boy took it all in his stride, showing no sign of suffering despite

Left: the Hindu holy man, Sai Baba of Shirdi, who died in 1918. Satyanarayana Raju, born in 1926, 'became' Sai Baba after suffering the physical trauma of a scorpion sting when he was 13. On a visit to Shirdi he recognised the first Sai Baba's friends although he had never met them in his present life

of Satya, eight years later, but many were sceptical of his claim.

Eventually someone challenged him to prove that he really was who he claimed to be. 'Bring me those jasmine flowers,' he ordered. Then he threw them on the floor. To everyone's amazement they landed in such a way that they spelt 'Sai Baba'.

In time, Satya came face to face with devotees of Sai Baba of Shirdi and he invariably recognised them. On one occasion, he took a photograph from someone, looked at it, and named the person it pictured – though it was a man Satya had never met. He then named the man and said he was the visitor's uncle – 'your father's elder brother, and my old devotee at Shirdi'.

For many people, however, it does not matter whether Satya Sai Baba is a reincarnation or not. The miracles he now performs leave them in no doubt that he is a very special person. A recurring miracle is the materialisation of holy ash (vibhuti), sometimes scooped from the air and sprinkled into the hands of visitors, but at other times made to pour out of an empty upturned urn into which his hand has been placed.

This ash has a variety of uses. He tells many of his followers to eat it, and it is reputed to have cured many ailments.

But it is the materialisation of solid objects which stretches belief to its limit. Sceptics argue that any competent stage conjuror can make objects apparently appear from nowhere, but Sai Baba's talents – if we accept the numerous testimonies that have been made – are in a very different league. Often

the ghastly treatment administered to him by the exorcist.

Then, one morning while his father was at work at his store, Satya called the rest of the family together. He waved his hand in front of them and produced candy and flowers. When the neighbours heard what had happened they crowded in and Satya obliged by producing candy and flowers for them, too.

News of these 'conjuring tricks' reached his father who was so incensed that he found a stout stick and went to the house to chastise his wayward son. 'This is too much! It must stop!' he shouted when he confronted Satya. 'What are you? Tell me – a ghost, a god, or a madcap?'

Satya replied simply: 'I am Sai Baba.' Then, addressing everyone present, he continued: 'I have come to ward off your troubles; keep your houses clean and pure.'

The reply was hardly helpful. The Raju family did not know of anyone named Sai Baba, but others in the village had heard of such a person: a Hindu holy man who performed many miracles, including healing the sick with ash from a fire which he had kept burning constantly at a mosque in Shirdi. He died in 1918 but he told his followers that he would be born again. That promise, it seems, was fulfilled with the birth

Above: a holy medallion created by Sai Baba. On one side (left) is the image of Sai Baba of Shirdi, on the other (right) the AUM symbol, signifying the word of creation. Baba says 'to hear that sound one has to approach as near as possible, the core of one's being . . . the Truth is AUM'

he invites people to name what they would like – then plucks it out of the air, or the 'Sai Stores' as he jokingly calls the invisible dimension from which it suddenly appears.

Howard Murphet, author of Sai Baba, man of miracles, tells of an occasion when Sai Baba asked him the year of his birth and then said he would get for him an American coin minted in that year.

He began to circle his down-turned hand in the air in front of us, making perhaps half a dozen small circles, saying the while 'It's coming now . . . coming . . . here it is!' Then he closed his hand and held it before me, smiling as if enjoying my eager expectancy. When the coin dropped from his hand to mine, I noticed first that it was heavy and golden. On closer examination I found, to my delight, that it was a genuine milled American ten-dollar coin, with the year of my birth stamped beneath a profile head of the Statue of Liberty.

Among the many reports which Murphet collected for his book is one by Mrs Nagamani Pourniya, widow of a Government District Transport Officer, who told him of a visit she and a small group of followers paid to the sands of the Chitravati river with Sai Baba. Instead of plunging his hands into the sands to produce materialised objects – which is a method he frequently uses – the miracle man simply scraped away sand to reveal buried objects. These proved to be statuettes, which then slowly rose out of the sand 'as if driven up by some power beneath'.

Hard to believe? Yes, but Christians are asked to believe that Jesus Christ worked many similar miracles.

Christians who accept the raising of Lazarus should not find it difficult to believe the story of V. Radhakrishna, a 60-year-old factory owner who visited Sai Baba's Puttaparti headquarters in 1953 in the hope of finding relief from the severe gastric ulcers that were making his life a misery.

He was given a room and spent all his time

Above: three forms of *avatar* – or gods incarnate – from the Indian pantheon. Sai Baba is believed to be an avatar

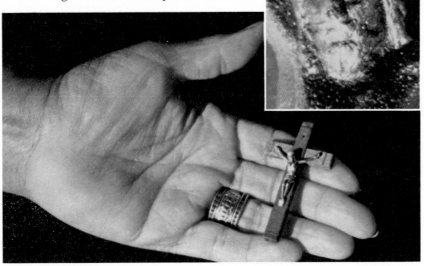

in bed, waiting for a visit from Sai Baba. When that came, the holy man made no attempt to cure him. He just laughed when Radhakrishna said he would rather die than go on suffering, and left the room without making any promises.

Eventually, the man's condition got worse and he went into a coma. When Sai Baba learned of this he said to the man's wife, 'Don't worry. Everything will be all right.' But when there was no improvement next

Above: Sai Baba often materialises crucifixes for his Christian friends

Inset: detail of a crucifix, said to show Jesus at the point of death. Sai Baba reveres Christ as a Master who came to unite all men through peace, sacrificing himself to atone for their violence and aggression

day the sick man's son-in-law sent for a male nurse who said the patient was so near death there was no hope of saving him. An hour later Radhakrishna became very cold and his family heard what they took to be the 'death rattle' in his throat. Slowly he turned blue and stiff.

When told what had happened, Sai Baba laughed. And when he visited the room to see the man's condition for himself he left without saying a word.

By the morning of the third day the body was even more corpselike: it was dark, cold and beginning to smell of decomposition. Some people advised the family to have it removed, but when Mrs Radhakrishna told Sai Baba this he replied: 'Do not listen to them, and have no fear; I am here.'

Eventually, Sai Baba went to the room again and found the family distraught. He asked them to leave and remained with the body for a few minutes. Then he opened the door and called them in. To their great relief and astonishment they found the 'dead' man conscious and smiling. Next day he was strong enough to walk and the gastric ulcers were found to be completely cured, never to return.

Such miracles are said to be the least important part of his work. He refers to his psychic phenomena as 'small items.' His mission is to attract attention to his spiritual teachings – to lead Man away from violence and hatred towards compassion and higher consciousness, and to unite many religions. He explains it this way: 'I give you what you want in order that you may want what I have come to give.' And that, he says, is to avert a nuclear holocaust.

But his incarnations as Sai Baba of Shirdi and Satya Sai Baba will not be enough to achieve that aim. He has already said he will be born again, as Prema Sai, in the 21st century in order to complete his mission.

Brahan Seer

In the 17th century, Kenneth Odhar – the prophet of the Seaforth family – was hailed as one of the greatest Highland seers ever. And, as FRANK SMYTH explains, it seems that his predictions continue to be fulfilled today

IF WE ARE to give folklore and historical legend any credence at all, the power of 'second sight' has been commonplace in the Highlands of Scotland – and in Ireland whence the Celtic people of the north came – for centuries. Until the 18th century, every glen and braeside from Lochaber to the far tip of Caithness had, it would seem, its resident 'wise' man or woman, traditionally the seventh child of a seventh child, who through the power of God or fairies inherited the gift of *taibh-searachd* – prophecy.

After the last Jacobite uprising ended with the disastrous battle of Culloden in 1746, the clans were considerably reduced in number and their remnants exiled and scattered to the West Indies, North America, and later Australia and New Zealand. But the tradition of the 'Highland seer' lived on; even today his descendants are looked upon tolerantly and with respect.

In the 19th century there was a quickening of interest in the 'romantic' Highlands. George IV encouraged the trend by appearing at Edinburgh with his portly frame wrapped in the newly invented 'Royal Stewart' tartan, a fashion followed by the Prince Consort, who went as far as to design a tartan wallpaper and carpet for Balmoral, and Sir Walter Scott had already fanned the flame with his popular historical novels.

In the wake of this 'romanticism' came the folklorists, indefatigably tramping over the heather in search of quaint tales and superstitions. One of the more respected of these

Baile-na-Cille in Uig on the Isle of Lewis, reputedly the place where Kenneth Odhar, the Brahan seer, received his precognitive powers. According to legend, he either found or was given a magic stone, and it was in this that he was able to see the future. It seems that Kenneth paid dearly for his gift, for one tale has him half-blinded, and several accounts describe him as 'cam' – one-eyed or squinting

was Andrew Lang, himself a Scotsman, an active member of the Society for Psychical Research, and the author of, among other books, *The making of religion* (1898), which dealt with examples of second sight among primitive societies. Turning to his homeland, Lang examined the evidence for and against the powers of the native seers. In a paper published in 1899, he was able to 'unblushingly confess the belief that there probably are occasional instances of second sight, that is of "premonitions"'.

However, Lang urged that all the evidence in each individual case be considered, pointing out that the strongest cases must rest on prophecies that had been recorded before their 'fulfilment', thus ruling out the possibility of romantic hindsight. Obviously, the more explicit the prediction, the more convincing its detailed fulfilment would be.

Under these terms, the posthumous claims made for Coinneach Odhar of Mackenzie, the Brahan seer, stand up to considerable scrutiny. Famous in his lifetime as the resident prophet of the mighty Seaforth family, he came to be regarded as one of the most impressive Highland seers ever when, 150 years after his death, his predictions regarding the unusual circumstances of the family's extinction came precisely true.

Coinneach – Gaelic Kenneth – was born in the parish of Uig on the Isle of Lewis around the year 1600. According to Alexander Cameron of Lochmaddy, who chronicled many of the seer's prophecies some years after his death, it was at some time during his early teens that Kenneth's powers developed. Several versions of their origins exist, all involved with the supernatural. According to one, his mother, tending her cattle in the graveyard of Baile-na-Cille near Uig, met

Prophet by appointment

the ghost of a daughter of the King of Norway, who gave her a blue stone in which Kenneth would see the future. Other accounts tell how Kenneth himself was given a white stone with a hole in it by the fairies, and it was through this that he was able to see coming events.

Whatever the source of his powers, news of them spread to Kenneth's feudal overlord, Kenneth Cabarfeidh – Staghead – Mackenzie, who in 1609 had been created first Lord Mackenzie of Kintail. The chief's stronghold was Brahan Castle, a few miles from Dingwall on the Cromarty Firth, and at his summons Kenneth Odhar went to live on the Brahan lands. Soon after Odhar's arrival the old chief died and was succeeded by his son, who was created first Earl of Seaforth in

Above: the writer and psychical researcher Andrew Lang (1844–1912), who examined the evidence for second sight in his native Scotland. He confessed to a belief in the existence of 'premonitions', saying: 'I know too many examples among persons of my acquaintance . . . to have any doubt about the matter'

Left: a *taibhsear* – seer – of the Highlands. Such figures commanded respect in the community as it was widely believed that the power of second sight was a gift from God, or inherited from the fairies

Below: the battle of Culloden, 1746, which – in one of his more memorable prophecies – the Brahan seer accurately predicted over 100 years before

1623; it was the first Earl's grandson who was to build Odhar's fame.

Kenneth, third Earl of Seaforth, was roughly the same age as Kenneth the poor prophet and seems to have been fascinated by him. He released the seer from his job as farm labourer on the Brahan estate and, although still lodged in a sod-roofed cottage, Odhar the Lewisman – who spoke only Gaelic – was introduced into local learned society.

He cannot have been a cheerful companion, for his predictions invariably involved bloodshed or disaster, pronounced with a dour relish. On one occasion, for instance, an elderly man, Duncan Macrae of Glenshiel, asked the seer to tell him 'by what means he would end his days'. Odhar immediately replied that he would die by the sword. Such an event seemed so unlikely that Odhar stood in danger of being discredited:

for one thing, Macrae had been distinguished in the Mackenzie army in clan wars without coming to harm, and for another there had been no tribal feuding for years. Nevertheless, recorded his kinsman and contemporary the Reverend John Macrae of Dingwall, Duncan Macrae died as predicted, the victim of a misunderstanding. In 1654 General Monck led a troop of Parliamentary soldiers up to Kintail and a company of them met Macrae walking in the hills behind his house. Addressed in a language he did not understand and startled by the strange uniforms, Macrae put his hand to his broadsword and was immediately cut down: 'This was all the blood that General Monck or his soldiers, amounting to 1500 men, had drawn.'

The weeping widow

Most of the time the seer's advice was unsolicited, and his predictions were interesting only because they proved accurate. One day he announced that 'A Lochalsh woman shall weep over the grave of a Frenchman in the burying place of Lochalsh.' Frenchmen were virtually unknown north of Edinburgh, and yet within a few months the Earl of Seaforth discovered that a Lochalsh woman had married a French footman who died young; the widow had taken to weeping by his graveside every day.

Doubtless these insights into the immediate future enthralled Odhar's contemporaries, but it was his long range predictions that fascinated the likes of Andrew Lang. Odhar gained nothing from them personally, not even prestige, for their fulfilment lay far in the future, and this as much as their accuracy gives them the hallmark of genuine precognition.

One pronouncement that was marvelled at when it proved true was that in the village of Baile Mhuilinn, in the west of Sutherland, there would live a woman named Baraball n'ic Coinnich (Annabella Mackenzie) who would die of measles. In about 1860 there was a woman of that name living in the

land but, said Kenneth, one day it would 'be under lock and key, and the Fairies secured within'. In the mid 19th century it became a cemetery, and today is surrounded by a fence with a locked gate.

For the Mackenzies of Fairburn, cousins of Seaforth, Odhar could see nothing but doom. Over the years he predicted gruesome fates for them, combined with financial ruin and final obliteration; eventually, Odhar said, a rowan tree would grow from a crack in Fairburn Tower, and a cow would calve in its upmost chamber. In Odhar's time the tower was new and strong, but in the 18th century, when its owners lost their lands following the Jacobite rebellion, it fell into ruin. In 1851 a cow did make its way up the narrow and precipitous stairway and calved in the top room, while a rowan tree sprang from a fissure half way up the tower wall and grew to a considerable size before dying in the summer drought of 1957.

village, but she was 95 years old and it seemed unlikely that her death would be caused by that disease; then, a few years later, Annabella died – as predicted – of measles.

In 1630 Seaforth 'lent' Odhar to a 'gentleman from Inverness', who wrote down a string of the seer's utterances. One well-authenticated pronouncement was made on the way to the gentleman's house. Crossing a bleak patch of moorland, Odhar said: 'Oh! Drummossie, thy bleak moor shall, ere many generations have passed away, be stained with the best blood of the Highlands. Glad I am that I will not see that day . . . heads will be lopped off by the score, and no mercy will be shown.' One hundred and sixteen years later the battle of Culloden was fought on that very spot.

Mystery of the moving stone
Another startling prediction concerned an 8-tonne stone that marked the boundaries of the estates of Culloden and Moray. The day would come, said Odhar, when the 'Stone of Petty' would be moved mysteriously from its position on dry land and re-erected in the sea of Petty Bay. It is a matter of record that during the stormy night of 20 February 1799 the huge stone was uprooted and ended in the sea some 250 yards (230 metres) from the shore line. No satisfactory explanation of its moving has ever been put forward.

In another of his predictions Odhar spoke of 'strings of black carriages, horseless and bridleless', which would pass through the Highlands, led by 'a fiery chariot' – a fair description of the railways of mid Victorian times. He also stated that ships with sails would pass behind the 'fairy hill' of Tomnahurich near Inverness; they began to do so when the Caledonian Canal was opened in the 1820s. Tomnahurich itself was common

Some of the seer's accurate predictions: of the common land at Tomnahurich that became a cemetery (above) in the 19th century, he said it would be 'under lock and key and the Fairies secured within'; of the advent of the railways (right) he said 'horseless' carriages would be led by a 'chariot of fire'; and the downfall of the Fairburn Mackenzies, he rightly said, would be signalled by the birth of a calf and the sprouting of a rowan tree in the ruin of Fairburn Tower (below)

Famous last words

When the mighty Seaforth family sentenced their resident seer to death, they also condemned themselves.

POPULAR FAITH in the prophecies of Kenneth Odhar, the most distinguished of Highland seers, was strong and widespread in the mid 17th century. Many of his predictions were well-known and were passed on from generation to generation: some came true in his lifetime, others long after his death; many are still unfulfilled.

Some of Odhar's prophecies may have been helped by his natural shrewdness. The strange, sulphurous waters of Strathpeffer, a few miles north of Brahan, had been shunned by locals as poisonous for years, but Odhar claimed that

Uninviting and disagreeable as it now is, with its thick crusted surface and unpleasant smell, the day will come when it shall be under lock and key, and crowds of pleasure and health seekers shall be seen thronging its portals, in their eagerness to get a draught of its waters.

In 1818, Strathpeffer became a fashionable spa, and the pump room, normally kept locked, is still a centre for health cures.

On the other hand, his prediction of a disastrous flood 'from a loch above Beauly', which would destroy a village in its vicinity, was unlikely in the extreme. There was no loch anywhere near Beauly, which stands at the innermost point of Beauly Firth. However, in the 20th century a dam was built across the river Conon at Torrachilty, a few

Right: the pump room at Strathpeffer mineral wells. The Brahan seer's prophecy that one day the waters would draw crowds of 'health seekers' astonished the local people, for it was popularly believed that the Devil himself washed there. However, in the late 18th century it was discovered that the waters had healing properties, and in 1818 Strathpeffer was established as a fashionable spa

Below: in 1966 heavy rain caused the hydro-electric dam at Torrachilty to overflow and this, in turn, caused the river Conon to burst its banks. The flooding created havoc in the village of Conon Bridge, destroying buildings, crops and cattle. The precise nature of this disaster had been foreseen, centuries before, by the Brahan seer

miles away from Beauly, and in 1966 it unexpectedly overflowed. The flood water killed hundreds of sheep and cattle, destroying grain, fences and buildings in the village of Conon Bridge, some 5 miles (8 kilometres) 'above Beauly'.

Odhar's end was surprisingly unforeseen, considering his gifts, but it did cause him to forecast with uncanny accuracy the end of his patron's line. Kenneth, third Earl of Seaforth, was a staunch Royalist who led a troop of his Mackenzie clansmen during the Civil Wars against Cromwell's army along the Scottish borders. After the death of Charles I he was imprisoned but, after the Restoration, was held in high esteem by Charles II, being granted extra lands and winning the hand of Isabella Mackenzie, sister of the Earl of Cromarty.

In the mid 1660s the Earl was sent to Paris by King Charles, and several months passed without Isabella receiving a letter from him. One night, Isabella asked the seer to tell her what her husband was doing. Odhar said that he saw him in a splendid room, well and happy, and 'indisposed' to return home yet. Isabella pressed him to tell her more, and the incautious prophet told her that the Earl was 'on his knees before a fair lady'.

The Countess immediately ordered the seer to be burned to death in a tar barrel as a

witch. Odhar was astonished and filled with
dismay at her reaction: he had expected
reward for his prophecies, not condem-
nation. But the Countess's decision was
upheld and, attended by representatives of
the Kirk, Odhar was taken to Chanonry
Point on the Moray Firth for execution.
There, he begged the ministers to write
down what he was going to say.

Speaking in his native Gaelic, he said that
he saw a Seaforth chief, the last of his house,
who would be deaf and dumb. He would
have four fair sons, all of whom he would
follow to the tomb. One of them would die on
the water. His daughter, whom the prophet
described as 'white hooded', would come
from lands to the east to live at Brahan, and
she would kill her sister. Thus all the
Seaforths would die. The seer continued:

And as a sign by which it may be known
that these things are coming to pass,
there shall be four great lairds in the
days of the last deaf and dumb Seaforth
– Gairloch, Chisholm, Grant, and
Raasay – of whom one shall be buck-
toothed, another hare-lipped, another

When Kenneth, third Earl of
Seaforth (left), patron of the
Brahan seer, was abroad on
business, his wife Isabella
(below), having had no
word from him, summoned
the seer to Brahan castle
(below left: the castle in
ruins) to give an account of
her husband. The seer told
her that he could see the Earl
with another woman, and
Isabella was furious.
Unfortunately for the seer,
she directed all her anger
against him and condemned
him to be burned as a witch

half-witted, and the fourth a
stammerer.

There would also be a laird of Tulloch, 'stag
like', who would kill four wives in succes-
sion, but the fifth would outlive him.

Odhar was executed near the modern
Chanonry Point lighthouse, by the road from
Fortrose to Fort George ferry; the place is
marked with a stone slab. But the memory –
and the implied threat – of his predictions
lived on, not least in the minds of the
Seaforth family. For the next hundred years
their fortunes fluctuated, and several of them
must have wondered if extinction were close
at hand. For their activities in the risings of
1715 the family were stripped of their titles,
but these were restored in 1726, and the
Seaforths subsequently became staunch

Hanoverians, growing richer and more
powerful by the year. The title of Earl of
Seaforth died out with its holder in 1781, but
the chieftainship passed to a second cousin
who seemed destined to bring even greater
honours to Brahan.

Francis Humberstone Mackenzie was
born in 1754 and early in his life became
member of parliament for Ross and Lord
Lieutenant of the county. During the re-
volutionary wars with France he raised a
regiment that subsequently became the
Seaforth Highlanders, and in 1797 he was
created Baron Seaforth of Kintail. In 1800 he
became Governor of Barbados, and in 1808
he was promoted to Lieutenant-General of
the army. As well as his military interest,
Seaforth was an amateur painter of great

having another 30 illegitimate offspring in Tulloch gained him the nickname 'the stag'.

Odhar's final prophecy came true within a few years of Seaforth's death. His eldest surviving daughter Mary had married Admiral Sir Samuel Hood in 1804; and when Hood died at about the same time as Seaforth while commanding the East Indian station, Mary returned home in widow's weeds to take over her father's lands: this formal dress included a white hood – so that she was both 'hooded' in fact, as Odhar had said she would be, and 'Hood' by name. One day she was driving her younger sister, the Hon. Caroline Mackenzie, through the woods by Brahan Castle when the ponies bolted and the carriage overturned; Lady Hood was merely bruised, but her sister died of her injuries.

The prophecies of the Brahan seer form a perennial guessing game for those Highlanders who know of them, for from time to time they still appear to come true – as in the case of the Conon Bridge disaster. One of the

talent, and he sponsored not only Sir Walter Scott, but also the painter Sir Thomas Lawrence and the scientist Sir Humphry Davy in their early years. He was happily married to the niece of Lord Carysfort, who bore him four sons and six daughters; altogether he presented a picture of enduring, well-established worth.

But the truth of the matter was that the prophet's predictions had begun to come true for Seaforth when he was 12 years old. In that year an outbreak of scarlet fever at his boarding school killed several of his fellow pupils and rendered Seaforth totally deaf; over the years his speech became affected, and towards the end of his life he could communicate only by making signs or writing notes.

His eldest son William Frederick died as a baby in 1786 and eight years later his second son George died at the age of six. His third son, Francis, a midshipman in the Royal Navy, was killed in his eighteenth year in a skirmish at sea – 'dying on the water', as Kenneth had foretold, in November 1813. Finally his last son, another William Frederick, the 24-year-old MP for Ross, died suddenly in August 1814. Seaforth himself died in January of the following year and was buried with his ancestors at Fortrose Cathedral. His contemporaries and neighbours, as the *Edinburgh Daily Review* pointed out in Seaforth's obituary, were the buck-toothed Sir Hector Mackenzie of Gairloch, the harelipped Chisholm of Chisholm, the retarded Laird Grant, and the stammering Macleod of Raasay. They also included Duncan Davidson, Laird of Tulloch, but it was to be many years before his part in the prophecy was fulfilled. When he died, Tulloch – then Lord Lieutenant of the county of Ross – had had five wives, four of whom had died in childbirth. Between them they had borne him 18 children, while his reputation for

Above: the stone at Chanonry Point, Fortrose, commemorating the 'legend of Coinneach Odhar, better known as the Brahan seer'. It was here that, in his final hour, the seer made his last prediction. 'I see far into the future,' he said, 'and I read the doom of the race of my oppressor. The long-descended line of Seaforth will, ere many generations have passed, end in extinction and sorrow. . . .' More than a century later, the Seaforth line came to an end just as the seer had foretold

Right: one of the seer's well-known proclamations concerned the depopulation of the Highlands, which began in the 18th century when many tenant farmers were evicted to make way for sheep on the land. This cartoon dates from the mid 19th century, when the problem was compounded by landowners charging high rents, forcing crofters to move south or, in many cases, emigrate

most remarkable of the seer's predictions related to the emptying of the Highlands of crofters in order to breed sheep. This came to pass with the Highland clearances of the mid 18th century. But the seer went on to say that those Highlanders driven away to far off lands as yet 'undiscovered or explored' would return to work in the Highlands in the days when the 'horrid black rains' should fall. Today, many Canadians, Texans and New Zealanders of Highland descent work in Scotland, notably in connection with offshore oil rigs and nuclear plants and submarine sites.

Naturally, the natives are curious: do the Brahan seer's 'black rains' – *siantan dubha* – refer to North Sea oil? Or do they refer to a fall-out of a much more sinister nature?

José Arigo

Arigo: surgeon extraordinary

He operated on the dying with only a rusty knife – and cured them. ROY STEMMAN looks at the extraordinary career of the humble Brazilian who performed surgical miracles 'under spirit guidance'

A PRIEST had arrived to administer extreme unction to the dying woman. Candles were lit and relatives and friends were gathered around her bedside in the town of Congonhas do Campo, Brazil. Her death, from cancer of the uterus, was expected at any moment.

Suddenly, one of those present rushed from the room, returning moments later with a large knife from the kitchen. He ordered everyone to stand back. Then, without warning, he pulled the sheets from the woman and plunged the knife into her vagina.

After several brutal twists of the blade he removed the knife and inserted his hand into the woman, withdrawing a huge tumour the size of a grapefruit. He dropped the knife and the bloody tumour into the kitchen sink, sat down on a chair and began to sob.

A relative rushed off to fetch a doctor; the rest stood silently as if transfixed by the astonishing scene they had witnessed. The patient was unperturbed: she had felt no pain during the 'operation' and the doctor confirmed that there was no haemorrhaging or other ill-effects. He also confirmed that the growth in the kitchen sink was a uterine tumour.

The extraordinary incident proved to be a turning point in the lives of the two people concerned. The woman recovered her health

Below: Arigo performs a delicate eye operation in his back parlour. Although it is the medium who goes into a trance, the patient feels no pain – nor, it seems, any fear, despite the unhygienic surroundings, primitive lighting and the complete lack of anaesthetics

completely. And the man who performed the 'surgery', José Arigo, found himself in great demand from people whose doctors had given them up as incurable patients. Yet he could not remember 'operating' on the woman.

Later, when such startling surgery became a daily occurrence in Congonhas do Campo – Arigo's home town – it was realised that he was in a trance when he treated the sick. His patients noticed he spoke with a German accent, and this was allegedly because Dr Adolphus Fritz, who died in 1918, was said to be 'operating' through him.

On most days when Arigo's clinic opened at 7 a.m. there was already a queue of 200 people waiting. Some he would treat in a rapid and often brutal fashion, pushing them against a wall, jabbing an unsterilised knife into them, then wiping it clean on his shirt. Yet they felt no pain or fear. There was very little blood, and the wound would knit together immediately and heal within a matter of days.

Not everyone received psychic surgery. For many he would simply glance at them, diagnose their problems without asking any questions, then write a prescription rapidly. The medicines prescribed were usually well-known drugs made by leading companies, but in large doses and combinations that were surprising according to conventional

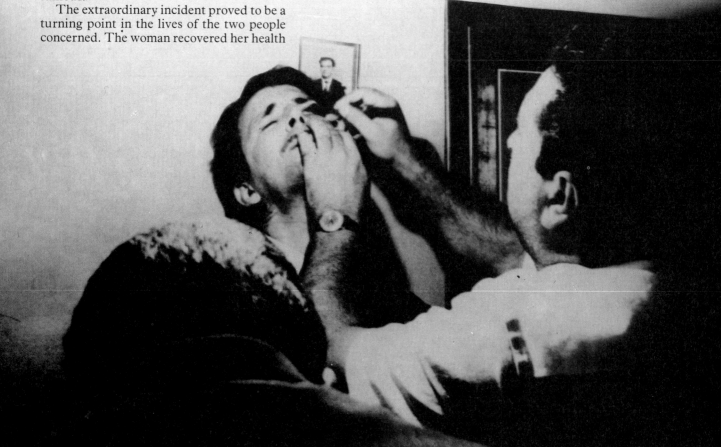

so in seconds and Dr Puharich was able to take the growth, and a film record of the surgery, back to the US for analysis.

In all the years that Arigo treated the sick by psychic surgery there was never a single allegation that his unconventional treatment caused anyone any harm. Nevertheless, what he was doing was frowned upon by the authorities because Arigo had no medical qualifications, and in 1956 he was charged with practising illegal medicine.

Many people were willing to testify that Arigo had cured them of serious illnesses, but their testimonies only gave ammunition to the prosecution case. Arigo was given a prison sentence, which was reduced to eight months on appeal, and was fined. But just before he was put into prison the Brazilian president, Kubitschek, gave him a pardon.

Eight years later he was charged again. Kubitschek was no longer president and Arigo was jailed for 16 months. After seven months he was freed, pending an appeal, but eventually had to serve a further two months in prison, in 1965. During both periods, the warden allowed him out of his cell to visit the sick and operate on them.

Arigo investigated

The man who had to hear that appeal was Judge Filippe Immesi, a Roman Catholic with little knowledge of Arigo. The more he studied the case the more difficult it became for him to make a decision without seeing the astonishing psychic surgery for himself.

One day, unannounced, he visited Congonhas do Campos with a friend who was a district attorney from another part of Brazil. Despite their anonymity Arigo recognised them immediately as representatives of the law and invited them to see the 'operations' from close quarters. He knew that he was breaking the law but thought the authorities might as well satisfy themselves that fraud was not taking place.

A near-blind woman with cataracts on both eyes was one of the first patients they saw being treated, and Arigo asked the judge to hold her head. Though he felt queasy he agreed to do so. John G. Fuller, author of *Arigo: Surgeon of the rusty knife*, quotes this testimony from Judge Immesi:

> I saw him pick up what looked like a pair of nail scissors. He wiped them on his sport shirt, and used no disinfectant of any kind. Then I saw him cut straight into the cornea of the patient's eye. She did not blench, although she was fully conscious. The cataract was out in a matter of seconds. The district attorney and I were speechless, amazed. Then Arigo said some kind of prayer as he held a piece of cotton in his hand. A few drops of liquid suddenly appeared on the cotton and he wiped the woman's eye with it. We saw this at close range. She was cured.

What Judge Immesi saw convinced him that

medical knowledge. Yet they cured people.

One conservative estimate suggests that he treated half a million patients in a five-year period. These included people from all walks of life: rich and poor alike, it made no difference to Arigo because he never accepted any money or gifts for his services.

During the 1950s and 1960s Arigo was a national hero in Brazil and hardly a day passed without newspapers headlining his latest healing miracles. Patients came from all over the world and he attracted the attention of Andrija Puharich, a New York researcher with a keen interest in the paranormal, who, after an initial visit, went back to Brazil with a team of doctors to investigate and film the phenomenon.

Puharich described the scene that first greeted him as 'a nightmare'. He wrote:

> These people step up – they're all sick. One had a big goitre. Arigo just picked up the paring knife, cut it open, popped the goitre out, slapped it in her hand, wiped the opening with a piece of dirty cotton, and off she went. It hardly bled at all.

Puharich was able to experience Arigo's extraordinary surgery for himself. He asked the Brazilian psychic surgeon to remove a small benign tumour from his arm. Arigo did

Above: José Arigo was put in jail twice for 'practising medicine illegally', but during both periods of imprisonment his jailers secretly let him out to perform operations on the sick – as successfully as ever

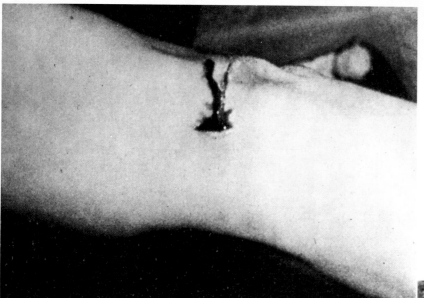

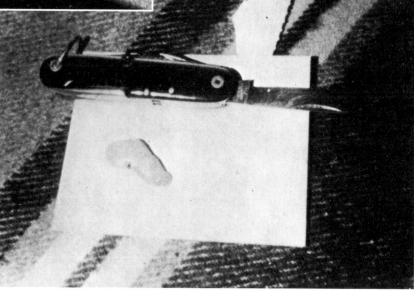

rushed to a São Paulo clinic with symptoms of intestinal obstruction. It was found that a tumour was blocking the transverse colon and a colostomy was performed.

Later she entered the Central Cancer Hospital in the same city for another operation, where it was found that the cancer had spread dramatically. Her weight had dropped by nearly half and the surgeon reported that she was totally beyond the resources of medical science.

So, as a last resort, she was taken to Arigo. Dr Madeiros accompanied the couple on the long trip to Congonhas do Campos and the dying woman had to be carried into the clinic. Being an Austrian, the husband spoke to 'Dr Fritz' in German and he replied in that language. Then Arigo glanced at the sick woman, scribbled a prescription, and said,

Arigo was a remarkable man who deserved to be the subject of scientific study. But the law was beyond doubt. What Arigo was doing was illegal and he would have to be punished – even though he was helping people. However, the judge looked for every possible excuse to reduce the sentence, with the result that Arigo was sent back to prison for just two months. While he was serving that sentence Arigo's case was under review by the Federal Supreme Court and it eventually decided to drop the charges against him. He was released on 8 November 1965.

The judge, of course, was not a medical man but he gave special attention to doctors' testimonies before reaching a verdict. And there were several who had had experience of Arigo's 'operations' and were prepared to say so in public. One of these was Dr Ary Lex, a distinguished Brazilian surgeon, a specialist in surgery of the stomach and digestive systems, lecturer at the Surgical Clinic of São Paulo University, and author of a standard textbook for Brazilian medical students.

Like Judge Immesi, Dr Lex was invited to hold a patient's head in his hands while Arigo operated. He witnessed four operations in half an hour and was satisfied that what Arigo was doing was paranormal. But he was not so impressed with the prescriptions. 'They were absolutely ridiculous,' he told author Guy Playfair. 'Some of them were for obsolete medicines which were only still being made because he prescribed them.' Some of them, he said, were also dangerous in the doses prescribed, and expensive.

However absurd the prescriptions may have seemed, their effects were frequently startling. Such a case concerned a young Polish woman whose body was riddled with cancer. She and her husband were friends of Dr José Hortencia de Madeiros, an X-ray specialist with the State Institute of Cardiology, who took a close interest in the case. The cancer was discovered when she was

Andrija Puharich, investigator of the paranormal, paid Arigo a visit to see the 'psychic surgeon' in action. He asked Arigo to remove the benign tumour (lipoma) from his arm and Arigo immediately made a deep incision (top) in the arm, then cut out the tumour with his unsterilised penknife (above)

'You take this, and get well.'

Dr Madeiros administered the abnormal dosage of drugs prescribed and she showed signs of improvement within a week. After six weeks her weight had returned to normal. She returned to Arigo who announced that she was out of danger and gave her two more prescriptions. On a third visit to the psychic surgeon, the patient was told that she was completely healed and he advised her to 'undo the operation' – a reference to the colostomy that enabled the body's waste to be passed through the abdomen into a bag. Arrangements were made for the operation to be reversed, and when her abdomen was opened the surgeons confirmed that all signs of cancer had vanished.

Arigo was killed in a car crash in January, 1971 – having told several people that he would not see them again – and the techniques he used to cure the sick remain a mystery. Arigo himself offered no explanation except to give credit to Jesus and Dr Fritz. And when he once saw a film of himself performing operations . . . he fainted.

Margo Williams

Medium Margo Williams claims to receive, through dictation by the dead, pleas for help, which she regards as her special mission to fulfil. But, asks ROY STEMMAN, how convincing are these 'spirit' messages?

ONE BRIGHT spring morning in 1976, Margo Williams was busy in the kitchen of her home in Ventnor, Isle of Wight, when she was startled by a woman's voice saying, 'My name is Jane.'

Margo turned with alarm to see who had entered the house, but there was no one there. Immediately, however, she had an overwhelming urge to pick up a pencil and write down what her invisible guest said; but later she could make little sense of her notes.

'Jane' dictated another message two days later and she returned on over 70 further

Below: Farnham parish church in Surrey, where Margo Williams, accompanied by author Roy Stemman, received an automatically written script allegedly from the spirit of John Lacey, who was searching for his wife Ann. Later, a tablet (inset) was discovered in the church, giving the name John *Lacy* and his wife's name as Agnes

occasions, telling a little about herself each time. She was, she said, a housewife from the mid Victorian period and she had lived in a seaside town in Devon. Margo's husband Wally began researching the scripts to see if he could verify the information given by their 'spirit' guest. When Jane said her family doctor's name was Mackenzie, Wally wrote to the Wellcome Medical History Library and discovered that there had been a doctor of that name with a practice in Sidmouth, Devon, at the time Jane said she had been alive. This, said Wally, 'fitted the facts perfectly'.

By this time Jane had been joined by numerous other communicators. 'We've had people from all walks of life,' Wally explains. 'Men and women, from humble servants to the top brass of the world in different forms.

Whispers from the past

There have been civilians, military, clergy, doctors – you name it, we've had it: an ever-increasing variety. At first it was very much a Victorian thing, but the time zone has extended and we have even heard from a woman called Margaret who died just after AD 1500.'

These voices from the past are known to psychical researchers as 'drop-in' communicators because they appear without rhyme or reason – unlike the 'spirits' of seances who apparently return to speak to their relatives or friends. But if the dead really were dictating Margo Williams's scripts, why were they doing it? Or could it be that the medium was deluding herself into believing that she was in touch with the next world?

It is not easy to answer these questions on the evidence of the scripts alone. If the information they contain is proved accurate by research, then critics could rightly suggest that the medium or her husband may have acquired that information normally and presented it as 'spirit messages'. Or perhaps Margo had read the information earlier in her life and forgotten it, and it was now being dredged up by her subconscious in the form of scripts.

I first met Margo in 1978 and was impressed by her sincerity and down-to-earth attitude to the phenomena. Wally, on the other hand, seemed to over-emphasise its importance, seeing great significance in every enigmatic word or odd coincidence.

During this meeting we discussed Appuldurcombe House, a ruin near Wroxall, on the Isle of Wight. The house is not said to be haunted, but when Mrs Jenny Gibbons, a friend of the Williamses, visited the place she felt very uneasy and decided to ask Margo and Wally if they could pick up anything psychically.

Soon after arriving at the ruin, on 24 June 1978, Margo heard a woman's voice and began writing. The script is typical of those

received by the medium:

Please, please, hear me. He desired me. He said I was comely. I was but a dairymaid here. Please, please, I have waited so long, so long. Old Targett, my father. Been here for years. Please, please hear me. His tongue as sweet as honey, so pleading with me. I met him by the big clump of trees where he deflowered me.

Richard, where are you? Please help me, please, please. My baby I called Thomas. Please, please help me to find him. He cared not how I fared after he gave me some money. My pa was so upset. Please, please, I try to look for

Margo Williams receives a script in the grounds of Waverley Abbey, Surrey. The communicator claimed to be a young woman who had lived in Waverley Abbey House, a mansion nearby. Like many automatic scripts, the information given was insufficient to provide the basis for a detailed investigation

him. . . . Until I find Richard I will stay by the house for eternity. Please help me find Richard. . . . 'Ee called me Mary, where art'ee Richard? 'Ee was the only one who called me Mary. . . .

Moved by her plea, the Williamses conducted their own research to see if Mary Targett really existed. They were almost at the point of giving up when Wally discovered a book entitled *The Oglander memoirs* in which there was a chapter headed 'Ye history of ye Worsley family', written by Sir John Oglander (1595–1648). Reading through the chapter, Wally found an account of a man named Richard Worsley, who was the equivalent of governor of the island around 1550; he had produced a bastard son Thomas by a dairymaid, Mary Targett.

A spirit found

On discovering that Richard Worsley had died in 1565 and was buried on the Isle of Wight at Godshill, Wally went with Margo and Jenny Gibbons in search of his grave. And the ghost of Mary Targett apparently went with them. For, in the church, using Richard's tomb as a writing table, Margo received a final, poignant message from the ghost of Appuldurcombe House: 'I have found 'ee Richard! Thank 'ee, thank 'ee. I can go onwards. Richard I love 'ee.'

This reunion reduced the three earthly 'witnesses' to tears. Sceptics, however, would remain unimpressed. Perhaps the Williamses had concocted the whole thing, or Margo had read about Mary Targett in some other book.

During the next eight months Margo visited many other sites, taking dictation from 33 earthbound spirits, 12 of whom were subsequently identified by Wally. Several of them announced that they had been 'released' by the Williamses' intervention.

Here, it seemed, was something that could be put to the test. I invited Margo and her husband to visit the mainland and join me on a ghost hunt in Hampshire and Surrey – a challenge they readily accepted. I selected a number of places to visit, some of which were reputedly haunted and others that, as far as I knew, had no ghosts at all. I did not tell the Williamses where I was taking them.

We went first to the ruin of Waverley Abbey, which had been founded in 1128 by the White Monks of the Cistercian Order. Margo wandered through the remains of the abbey, then began to write furiously in her notebook; the communicator was a young woman who claimed to have lived in Waverley Abbey House.

At the parish church of Farnham, Margo received a script from one John Lacey, who was searching for his wife Ann. And while we were taking a pub lunch, at the William Cobbett in Farnham, the ghost of Sir Reginald Bloomfield 'appeared'. He revealed that he had designed the chancel of an

the wall of the church we found a stone tablet recording the death of 'Mr John Lacy' (note the different spelling) on 6 October 1766. But Margo had walked past the stone before receiving the script, so she could have seen the inscription, consciously or subconsciously. The tablet also recorded the death of Lacy's wife Agnes in 1784. Margo's script referred to the wife as Ann.

In the William Cobbett pub, Sir Reginald Bloomfield interrupted our lunch to tell us about a lady love he had visited there. He mentioned designing a church chancel. The man concerned was easy to identify, even though the spelling of his name was incorrect: it should have been Blomfield. He was a noted church architect in the Surrey and Hampshire area and his name is to be found in most reference books relating to southern England. Strange, then, that he should 'appear' in a pub. There was no way that we could verify his story. The same was true of the other communicators, who gave even fewer clues as to their identities.

Although that investigation failed to provide evidence that Margo Williams was in

unusual church some way away. 'I travelled in my carriage,' he said. 'The fair lady I had an assignation with was staying here. . . .'

I thought Farnborough Abbey in Hampshire might have a ghost or two. The bodies of Napoleon III and his wife, the Empress Eugénie, are in its vaults. The French Emperor came to England after he was deposed in 1871, dying two years later at Chislehurst in Kent. While Wally and I discussed the history of the abbey with a guide, Margo found a quiet corner where she received a script from one of her regular communicators, Captain Charles Bennett. 'There are bodies where no souls dwell now,' he told us, adding that the Empress was now living another life on earth.

Our final visit was to Mytchett Place, which is occupied by the Royal Army Medical Corps. I knew that a variety of ghostly happenings had been reported in recent times, and that Rudolph Hess, Hitler's deputy, was imprisoned there during the war, after he had parachuted into Scotland on an unsuccessful peace mission. I told Margo nothing. The communication she received was from a man who had stayed there, at an unspecified date, and had been burned after a cigar fell on his bed sheets.

Rather than visit more sites, we agreed that Margo would return to some of those already mentioned in the hope that she would receive more information, and more scripts were produced.

So had Margo Williams's scripts proved her claim that the dead were communicating with her? I had to conclude that, on this occasion, they had not.

At only two of the locations did a communicator provide a full name. 'John Lacey' dictated his message at Farnham church. On

Above: Margo in front of Waverley Abbey House

Right: Margo receives a script in the William Cobbett public house, Farnham. It was here that a Sir Reginald Bloomfield communicated; he said he had met a lady love there and that he had designed a church chancel. Sir Reginald *Blom*field was a noted architect who had lived in the area and designed many churches there. Most reference books about Surrey and Hampshire mention him, and Margo could easily have read about him – yet who is to say that this communication is not genuine?

touch with various spirits, this does not necessarily mean that the information in her scripts was not obtained paranormally. Late in 1979 Margo's psychic talents became more varied; to include healing and physical manifestations – a silver glitter appeared on her hands and body when she was 'achieving release of earthbound spirits'. Perhaps investigation of these facets of her work will provide proof of her paranormal powers.

But for the time being, the intriguing case of Margo Williams serves to show just how difficult it is at times to prove – or disprove – mediums' claims.

Coral Polge

Coral Polge has the remarkable talent of being able to draw exact likenesses of people she has never seen or known – people whose faces come to her from beyond the grave through her psychic powers. ROY STEMMAN describes an extraordinary medium

MANY THOUSANDS of people believe they have received tangible proof of life after death. It has been given to them in the form of portraits of their loved ones, drawn by a London medium, Coral Polge.

These pencil and pastel sketches, which now adorn walls in homes around the world, often show a striking likeness to dead relatives and friends. Not only are their features recognisable but sometimes they are dressed in a characteristic style.

Psychic artist Coral Polge, wife of spiritual healer Tom Johanson, does not see the dead, nor is her hand controlled by spirits in the way that automatic writing mediums claim to receive their scripts. 'I just "feel" the people coming through,' Coral told the Spiritualist newspaper *Psychic News* in 1972. 'I know exactly what to draw without thinking about it. It's involuntary, like breathing or walking.'

In the early stages of her career Coral gleaned the information for her portraits by holding letters written to her by those anxious to discover the fate of people near to them who had died; nowadays she concentrates on personal sittings, enabling enquirers to see the sketches as she produces them. She also demonstrates her remarkable talent in public, using an overhead projector so that large audiences can witness the drawings being made.

It was during one of these public performances that Coral drew the features of an elderly man with a droopy moustache. Among those in the audience was Phyllis Timms of Salisbury, Wiltshire, who recognised the man as her grandfather, Herbert Light, who had died of cancer.

But Mrs Timms did not acknowledge the portrait immediately: she wanted 'absolute proof'. In addition to drawing likenesses of the dead, Coral Polge also picks up psychic impressions that help to confirm their identity. In this case, she announced that she felt the elderly man was related to someone in the audience in a green dress. No one responded, and Mrs Timms was not wearing green. The psychic artist was insistent, however, that green was important as a link with the man she had drawn. It then occurred to Mrs Timms that her maiden name was Green – and she raised her hand to accept the portrait.

Coral's introduction to Spiritualism came through her parents, both of whom received spiritual healing in the 1940s. Then, during a visit to Harrow Spiritualist Church, she was

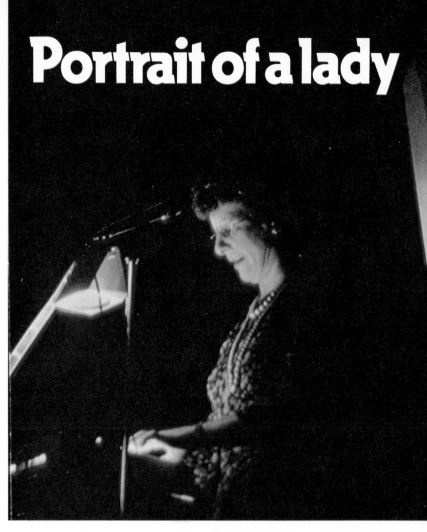

Portrait of a lady

Above: Coral Polge often gives public demonstrations of her skills as a psychic artist by projecting her drawing on an overhead screen while working on it. This example was made in Australia in 1980

Right: drawings made by Coral Polge compared with pictures of the subjects. She produces her sketches in a matter of minutes – which makes her ability to capture her unseen 'communicators' all the more remarkable. Sometimes the results are unexpected, as one sitter discovered. She was hoping for a portrait of former UN Secretary-General Dag Hammarskjöld, whose biography she was writing. When Coral drew a 'pretty little girl' the sitter was disappointed – until she remembered a family portrait that showed that Coral's depiction of Hammarskjöld was in fact very accurate (far right, top)

Above: Coral Polge's drawing, made at a public demonstration, of a man called Herbert Light (above right). Light's grand-daughter, who was in the audience, recognised his features immediately. But it was only after Coral had given further information – which could not have been acquired by normal means – that she acknowledged the portrait

told by a medium that she would be a psychic artist. Coral was trained as an artist at Harrow Art School, but she confesses that she was then hopeless at portraits – her particular interest was textile design; never-theless, the medium's prediction was not met with scepticism: 'I never had any doubts this was what I had been looking for.'

Coral took her first psychic circle in 1950, and in the next two decades produced an estimated 35,000 portraits.

To begin with, many of the people she drew were spirit guides – Red Indians, nuns, wise Chinese, smiling monks – and although they pleased the sitters they did not provide definite proof of survival, for no one could positively identify the subjects as having once lived on earth. So Coral made a special effort to produce more portraits of relatives. The results can sometimes be very impress-ive; it is not unusual for a sitter to burst into tears as he or she sees recognisable features appear on the psychic artist's pad. 'If I never get any more evidence for as long as I live, this is enough to convince me Spiritualism is true,' one woman told Coral.

High expectations

Coral cannot produce portraits to order. 'It creates barriers when people come expecting or wanting me to draw someone in particular. I draw whoever is able to get through.' Yet people do visit her with high expectations, sometimes raised by messages from dead relatives that they have received through other mediums.

One such visitor, who went to see Coral Polge anonymously, was expecting a portrait of a 'special person'. What Coral did not know was that the woman was writing a biography of Swedish-born Dag Ham-marskjöld, the former United Nations Secretary-General who died in an aeroplane crash in Africa in 1961. The woman had a keen interest in Spiritualism and had ap-parently received several communications from the statesman through other mediums;

Left: a drawing by Coral Polge of the celebrated opera singer Maria Malibran compared to a portrait from life (right). In this case the picture was not produced for a relative, but for another singer

Below: a portrait of a spirit guide. In the early part of her career Coral Polge often drew spirit guides, but this meant little to those who wanted to communicate with someone known to them. She then made a special effort to sense her sitters' relatives trying to 'come through'

in one of these he promised her a portrait if she visited a psychic artist.

It was therefore with some disappointment that she watched as Coral drew a pretty little girl. At first she thought the sitting was a failure, but slowly, as the portrait took shape, it began to look strangely familiar. Soon she was smiling with pleasure: Hammarskjöld *had* produced his portrait after all.

While researching her book, the woman had looked at many old family photographs. One, she recalled, showed Dag Hammarskjöld at the age of two, sitting on his mother's knee, with long hair and wearing a dress. He looks just like a pretty little girl.

From singer to singer

A portrait produced by Coral Polge also provided corroboration of spirit messages received by singer Grace Brooks. When Grace visited the psychic artist she received a portrait of a young woman with an unusual hair style. 'This is a Spanish singer named Maria,' Coral told her.

Grace had received messages from Maria through the automatic writing of a young Australian singer, Deidre Dehn, whom she met on the set of the film *Oliver!* At first, Maria had simply given Deidre her Christian name and the surname Garcia; later she supplied the name Malibran. Deidre discovered that Maria Malibran (*née* Garcia) had been a celebrated opera singer of Franco-Spanish descent. Born in Paris in 1808, she made her London début at the age of 17; she died in Manchester, aged 28, after a fall from a horse.

When Deidre Dehn returned to Australia, Grace Brooks believed her contact with Maria Malibran to be broken. But the link persisted, it seems. The drawing produced by Coral Polge is strikingly similar to a

portrait Grace found later at the British Museum.

The British medium has demonstrated her psychic art in various other European countries and in Canada and Australia. She has also made numerous television appearances. During a six-week tour of Australia in 1980 she was featured on the nationally broadcast *Don Lane Show*. On this occasion Coral was asked to draw just one portrait; she produced a picture of a young man, saying that he had three brothers and a father who was in poor health. A member of the studio audience recognised him immediately as the son of a friend; he had been killed in a car crash a year earlier.

Coral Polge also spent three weeks in Canada in 1980, during which time she gave 80 private sittings and several newspaper interviews and appeared in public twice, sharing the platform with another medium, David Young – she drawing the spirit communicators while he conveyed messages from them.

Not everyone accepts that Coral's drawings provide evidence of survival beyond the grave. Some regard them as extraordinary examples of extra-sensory perception, while sceptics dismiss them as coincidence. Not all the faces she draws are of the dead: she has occasionally produced portraits of babies before they were born. And she once did a drawing for a Norwegian television producer who was in Britain with a camera crew; he recognised the portrait immediately – it was of one member of the crew who had been unable to visit Britain at the last moment.

What does Coral Polge think of her strange gift? 'After producing so many drawings, you don't try to rationalise it,' she says. 'But I still feel a slight amazement that it has anything to do with me.'